Dave Barry

Biography
Laughing Through the Years

David Riley

TABLE OF CONTENTS

CHAPTER 1
MOM AND DAD

I was a baby at birth, just like a lot of people in the Baby Boom generation. About thirty miles north of New York City, in the town of Armonk, New York—yes, a hamlet—this incident took place in 1947. Armonk is a distinguished address today. It is home to IBM's global headquarters. The village is a wealthy hamlet with expensive real estate and a wealthy populace. In the modern world, it is impossible to hurl a rock in Armonk without striking a hedge fund manager.

When I was growing up, it wasn't. To the best of my memory, my buddies and I flung a lot of rocks—we didn't have video games—but we never struck someone who was wealthy.

There were about 2,000 people living in Armonk at the time, and almost everyone knew one another. Some residents were wealthy, while others commuted to the city for corporate work. However, there were also tradespeople and working-class families. Two carpenters and two plumbers were among our neighbors. This was lucky for my father, who was building our house and required a lot of help with plumbing and carpentry.

My father was a Presbyterian clergyman, not a builder. He was building our house since he lacked the funds to hire someone else to do it. He therefore completed the task himself, beginning with the hand excavation of the foundation.

Along the way, Dad learned how to build houses, although it wasn't always easy. He once spent a good portion of an afternoon trying, without success, to hang a door. When he eventually gave up, he sent me to the Petersons, our neighbors, to ask if Henry Peterson would be willing to consult. An elderly Swedish man named Henry was a superb carpenter and a friend of my father's.

Henry shook his head and exclaimed, "Dave, Dave, Dave," which sounded more like "Dafe, Dafe, Dafe" due to his Swedish accent, when he saw what Dad had done to the door. Within minutes, he skillfully hung the door after grabbing some tools. It is probably what my father hoped would occur.

The Petersons had a wonderful neighborhood. Mrs. Peterson was really kind, so I always went to them first when I had to sell candy for Little League. I detested having to make sales. "You don't want to buy any Little League candy, do you?" was my sales pitch. However, Mrs. Peterson consistently demanded that I sell her some.)

The Barry house was essentially a construction site during my boyhood, with incomplete walls and ceilings, building supplies strewn about, and the odd electrical wire protruding from someplace. Even though the house got better throughout the years, Dad never fully finished it—at least not while I lived there. He worked on it countless weekends and evenings.

Our home had peculiarities. Our water supply came from a well, and occasionally the water would stop flowing, requiring someone to prime the pump. Usually, I was in charge of this, especially when Dad was at work. I would get a lantern and head out to the pump house, a damp underground structure with low ceilings that housed the pump and about 400 trillion spiders. To get running water back, at least temporarily, I would go down there, unscrew the plug, pucker up, and blow air into pump. I fueled the pump countless times throughout the years. "Oh, YOU again," would be the spiders' reaction.

We shared a half-mile-long, one-lane dirt road with three other families. When it snowed, it was up to the families—the dads, really—to shovel the snow off our road because the town didn't maintain it. For many years, the method they employed involved attaching tire chains to someone's vehicle and using it to pull a handcrafted wooden plow in the shape of a V, which was supposed to push the snow to the sides of the road. This system wasn't very good. The automobile kept getting stuck, and the rope that pulled the plow kept snapping. As a result, the fathers spent a lot of time pushing the automobile, yelling directions to one another, getting flushed, occasionally using foul language, occasionally pausing to regain their breath, and, as fathers used to do whenever they had free time, lighting up cigarettes.

When I talk about the Barry homestead, I don't want to imply that I was raised in a poor, difficult situation. Absolutely not. Not even close. I had a great childhood, despite spiders. Despite having few material possessions, we had a great time. We were also free. We referred to the numerous sizable areas of undeveloped property behind our house as the Woods. Back then, the area was a vast, open nature preserve with many acres of forests, meadows, brooks, and ponds. Today, it is divided into well-kept McMansion estates.

If we local kids ventured onto the land, the landowners didn't mind, so we did. We explored, climbed trees, swung on vines, dammed creeks, swam in and skated on lakes and ponds, caught very poor frogs, shouted, burped, farted, and of course threw rocks, lots of rocks. We spent many pleasant hours wandering the woods.

We rode our bikes for miles around Armonk when we weren't in the woods, searching for adventures and other kids to play with or irritate. We played running bases, red rover, hide-and-seek, capture-the-flag, and other mutant baseball games with as few as two players per team and as many as fourteen. We had arguments from time to time. We used BB guns to shoot many things, including each other. As we grew older, we hitched rides to the movies in White Plains or Mount Kisco. In addition to trying cigarettes, we also got into what I shall euphemistically refer to as "mischief."

Needless to say, most of these activities were done without parental supervision. We Boomers have said this a lot, but it's true: Parents in those days frequently had no idea where or what their children were doing. Parents generally believed that everything was OK provided the children returned home by suppertime without suffering any serious injuries. It wasn't because our parents didn't love us; rather, I believe it was primarily that they didn't believe that the world was inherently hazardous. They had just returned from a world war and had grown up during the Depression. The 1950s weren't as frightening to them.

Parents were also very busy then. Mine were, anyway. My dad commuted to New York City to perform his actual job as executive director of the New York City Mission Society, a nonprofit that operated programs for inner-city children, when he wasn't building our house. He participated actively in the civil rights movement and the anti-poverty community in New York. He frequently worked late and on the weekends, attended neighborhood gatherings and meetings, and occasionally gave guest sermons at churches in Bedford-Stuyvesant, the Bronx, and Harlem.

His father was a minister in Minneapolis, Kansas, where my dad was born. Dad grew raised in Cleveland, where his father was assigned to a church when he was two years old. He attended Chicago Theological Seminary after attending Oberlin College. When Dad secured a job with the Presbyterian Board of National Missions in New York City, he married my mother, whom he had met in Chicago. They relocated to Armonk in search of space to raise a family because land there was inexpensive back then, and they boldly started their do-it-yourself home project.

Despite his shortcomings as a carpenter, my father was an excellent man. He dedicated his life to improving the lives of others and was wise, compassionate, and kind. People loved my dad, trusted him, confided in him, and relied on him because they recognized his kindness instinctively.

Although he didn't have a congregation because he wasn't a pastor, he was someone that people turned to in times of need. Our phone would frequently ring, and it would be someone who was crying, ill, having family issues, having a troubled child, or discussing suicide.

"Is Dave present?" they would ask.

For as long it took, Dad would go on the line, sit in the living room, smoke his Kent cigarettes, and listen—he was a superb listener—while speaking slowly, calmly, always calmly, providing what consolation he could, and never passing judgment. Day or night, Dad would put on his coat and hat and go out if they needed him. When someone needed him, he was there.

Despite being a devoted Christian, Dad did not hold people to his standards. He performed several weddings throughout the years, many of which were for individuals who did not identify as religious or whose religions forbade them from being married. He would marry Baptists to atheists and Jews to Catholics. He would marry someone if they were in love.

My father was anything but holy, but I'm making him seem that way. He never came across as arrogant, conceited, or smug. Around him, people were at ease. There was no clerical collar on him. He loved to make song parodies, drink, dance, and sing at gatherings. He enjoyed nearly all forms of humor. He had multiple editions of Robert Benchley's collected columns and was a devotee of the great humorist. I read those books when I was about eleven or twelve years old, and I became completely enamored with them. They undoubtedly inspired my writing, and I still read them now.

Dad's humor was self-deprecating. Because he accepted a job and never finished his thesis, he had a running joke about not having a PhD. He would say, "If only I had finished my PhD thesis!" while performing a menial home duty. I'm cleaning this toilet instead.

My dad loved to laugh. This is one of the reasons he married my mother.

"Where did you get your sense of humor?" is the question interviewers ask me the most throughout the years. My mother is always my response.

Mom's upbringing was harder than Dad's. Her family suffered throughout the Depression, but his was spared the worst. She was raised in a modest house with a sod roof after being born to low-income parents close to Longmont, Colorado. Her father found employment as a mechanic at a sugar-beet factory when she was about ten years old. The family relocated to Minatare, Nebraska, which is near Scotts Bluff.

Her home life was not cheerful. She didn't have a good relationship with her mother, whom she rarely mentioned and saw much less of in later life. She found Nebraska during the Depression to be depressing and dull, and she didn't have any pleasant recollections of it. "She missed Longmont and Colorado terribly because it was in the foothills of the Rockies and beautiful," remembers my brother Phil, our family historian: "But the Minatare and Scottsbluff area was flat plains and drab, and the wind whistled and howled at night, which she hated." She ridiculed Minatare living, claiming that the amusement consisted of attending funerals with her friend Gwen.

My mom's companion and conspirator was Gwen. They showed no deference to authority. As they frequently did, my mom would tell us about the day they got into trouble in high school and a teacher severely told them they would be staying after school for detention. With a voice full of happy expectation, Gwen turned to face my mother and said, "Oh, Marion, shall we?"

Mom cherished that recollection.

She left home once she was old enough to do so, and she never returned. She worked to pay for her education at the University of Nebraska. She relocated to Chicago after graduating, where she worked as a secretary for what would later be known as the Manhattan Project, albeit she was a low-level clerical employee and had no idea what that meant. Although she couldn't remember anything specific, she said that taking dictation from Enrico Fermi was the most memorable experience she had from that employment.

She first met my father in Chicago. Two humorous people in love eventually married because they made each other laugh.

They had four kids: me, my younger brother Phil, my older sister Kate, and my younger brother Sam. In many respects, my mother was a normal suburban housewife from the 1950s, raising a family full of children. She spent her long days cleaning, cooking a ton of food, packing school lunches, going grocery shopping, and dragging us around in the station wagon to Little League games, scout meetings, school functions, parties, etc. She threatened to turn the station wagon if we didn't stop punching each other. She appeared to be a typical mother of the era.

She was different from other mothers. She was sharp-witted, with a dark sense of humor that coiled inside her, ready to attack at any moment.

For instance, we Barry kids used to spend a lot of time at the pond in the woods behind our house. In the winter, we would ice skate there, and throughout the rest of the year, we would engage in basic pond games. I vividly recall going to the pond with my sister, Kate, on a summer day when I was around seven or eight. My mother, who was in the kitchen as usual, called out the window to inquire about our destination.

When we replied that we were heading to the pond, Mom yelled, "Don't drown, kids!" in the upbeat tone of a housewife from a 1950s TV advertisement.

"We won't!" we retorted with joy. We found it amusing. However, most mothers would never have made that joke.

When anything went wrong, she would often say, "Oh well, someday we'll all be dead." Everyone always felt better after doing this. It really did.

When Mom had errands to run around Armonk, like going to the drugstore, picking up the dry cleaners, or getting groceries, she would occasionally bring us along. The town's tradesmen regularly welcomed her. Ray Briccetti was manning the slicer behind the meat counter as usual as we entered Briccetti's market, and I recall him calling out, "Marion!" when he saw Mom. (Everyone referred to her as Marion.) "How are you?"

Mom said brightly, "Ray, you're just shitty!"

which Ray cherished. Unlike other buyers, she was unique.

Mom would remark, "I'm going to put on my bathrobe and pink curlers and drive right down to the school and give that teacher a PIECE OF MY MIND," if any of us Barry kids were having an issue, say with a teacher.

which she would never have done in reality, of course. In any case, it was beneficial since it was humorous. Even as grownups, Mom would threaten to resolve our issues by dressing in her bathrobe and curlers and going to confront the person causing them. And it was always helpful, in some small manner.

My friends adored my mom. When my roommate Rob Stavis came to visit us during a break when I was in college, he told Mom that he had recently been left by his fiancée and was experiencing severe depression. Mom listened thoughtfully and sympathetically, and she loved Rob. "She was a little snot," Mom added, placing a hand on Rob's arm after he finished. Rob laughed uncontrollably because he knew in his heart that she was correct.

Another example: My parents' friend used to send us a homemade fruitcake every Christmas. It should be obvious that no one in our family genuinely enjoyed fruitcake. Nevertheless, this thick slurry of holiday consideration made its way to our home each year, and eventually it became a treasured custom that involved my mother, me, and the kitchen door.

"Look, Davey!" she would say. "The fruitcake is here now!"

"Hurrah!" I would exclaim. "Hopefully, unlike last year, we don't unintentionally leave it in the kitchen doorway!" After that, I would put the fruitcake on the sill and open the kitchen door.

"Uh-oh!" my mother would exclaim. "It's becoming chilly! I should probably shut the kitchen door.

She would also smash the fruitcake's door. At times, it took multiple slams for her to finally end its suffering. We would then dispose of it in the trash pail. For at least a decade, we continued this custom, and it remains one of my favorite Christmas memories.

One final illustration: Tom Schroth, the editor of the Brooklyn Eagle, a now-defunct daily, lived next door to us in Armonk. Tom was a humorous, carefree man who grew to be my parents' close friend. My dad, who I mentioned was constantly attempting to build our house with little success, borrowed Tom's Skilsaw at one point.

Tom later relocated to Washington, DC, to work as the editor of Congressional Quarterly after the Eagle folded in 1955. The Skilsaw, however, was still at our house. Tom pretended to be furious and demanded that his Skilsaw be returned, which turned into a recurring joke between him and my parents. They've written about this topic for years.

Mom, who had been threatening to act on the Skilsaw matter for a while, finally did so shortly after my folks received that letter. Unbeknownst to Tom, she packed the Skilsaw and my five-year-old brother, Sam, into our car and made the little over 250-mile journey from Armonk to Washington, DC. Her only motivation was to ring Tom's doorbell that night so she could deliver him the saw and say, "Here's your goddamned Skilsaw," when he opened it and was completely taken aback to see her standing on his doorstep.

To my knowledge, no other mother ever did it.

My parents were a very excellent father who was also quite hilarious, and a very good mother who was also extremely funny. They provided us Barry kids with an amazing upbringing.

This does not mean they were perfect. Like everyone else, they had problems and both suffered in later years.

Dad became addicted to booze. This occurred while I was in my early twenties, after I had moved out. My parents were part of the Armonk social scene in the 1950s and 1960s, and drinking was a big part of that society. He had always enjoyed drinking. Almost every weekend, they and their friends organized or attended cocktail parties, some of which were quite crazy. However, Dad always appeared to be in control. He was never visibly intoxicated, at least not in my observation.

However, by his seventies, he was drinking much more, and eventually, he descended into complete alcoholism. People were noting that his drinking was interfering with his work. He started skipping appointments and being absent for extended periods of time. Mom knew he was intoxicated, even though he claimed he wasn't when he crashed his car. She feared that he would harm himself or someone.

I was employed at the Daily Local News, a newspaper in West Chester, Pennsylvania, when she called me at some point and asked if I could travel to New York City to speak with Dad about his drinking. I went even though I didn't want to. I paused outside Dad's door when I arrived at the City Mission offices to speak with his longtime secretary, who, like everyone who worked with him, adored him. She was sobbing as she told me how difficult it was to watch him in this state, occasionally slurring his words and occasionally nodding off at his desk.

I wasn't sure what to expect when I stepped in to see Dad, but he didn't appear or sound intoxicated. He pretended it was nothing more than a friendly visit, even though he knew why I was there. He didn't drink when he brought me to lunch at a nearby restaurant. Our lunch was uncomfortable. When I tried to question him about his drinking, he resisted, claiming that people were overreacting and that he didn't have a drinking problem in his cool, collected manner.

I didn't think he was real. He seemed evasive, which was not like the dad I knew, and I didn't think he was right. I tried to question him and expressed my opinions, but he calmly insisted that everything was fine and that he was fine. Eventually, I gave up. I was his son, a twentysomething child; he was my father, the wise man, the pillar of the family, the adored and esteemed Rev. Dr. Barry. Our dynamic was set in stone, and lunch was not going to change that. We returned to his office and exchanged farewell hugs, although they weren't very strong.

Then things got even worse. Dad was in another car accident. Mom was becoming frantic, worrying about herself and him, and occasionally even considering leaving him—something I couldn't imagine doing—but she was considering it.

She then called me one day to tell me that Dad was receiving assistance. When he reached his lowest point, he called a friend who was a member of Alcoholics Anonymous. After telling Dad to pack, the buddy came to the house and took him to a retreat for drying off, where he spent a few weeks. "I have Dave back," Mom told me when he got home.

A few months later I got a letter from Dad. I no longer have it, so this is paraphrasing, but it was something like I dimly remember, through my alcoholic haze, my son coming to see me, and trying to talk to me. I'm sorry you had to do that, and I'm sorry I didn't listen.

Dad was completing steps eight and nine of Alcoholics Anonymous' twelve-step program, which deal with making apologies. Dad was totally devoted to Alcoholics Anonymous; he consistently showed up to meetings and was sober for the remainder of his life.

He did more than that. He met Buford Peterson, a recovering alcoholic and former prisoner, through Alcoholics Anonymous. Buford had established the Fellowship Center, a program that offered prisoners alcoholism treatment. The majority of jails back then provided drug-addiction treatment, but there were frequently no programs for the many offenders who were imprisoned for alcohol-related offenses. After Dad became president of Fellowship Center, he worked to spread its programs across the New York State prison system during his remaining years. Dad and Buford became close friends and allies.

That was my father: not just addressing his personal issues and attempting to make amends for any wrongs he had committed, but also figuring out how to use his experience to benefit others and dedicating the remainder of his life to that goal. He was a decent man. I've never known a better man than him.

Unfortunately, he was not healthy. Even after quitting alcohol, he continued to smoke heavily for the most of his life, claiming that nicotine was a more difficult addiction to overcome. His cardiac problems finally caught up with him when he was in his mid-sixties. After being admitted to the hospital, the doctors stated there was nothing else to do and that he should die at home in the house he had constructed.

Mom called to tell me that Dad wasn't going to have much time left and to come to Armonk. I was still living in the Philadelphia suburbs in 1984, but I had just been hired by the Miami Herald to write a humor column for Tropic, their Sunday magazine. To see my dad, I drove home.

After that, I gave Tropic's editor, Gene Weingarten, a call to ask if I might write a non-humor piece about that most recent visit. I wrote a column called "A Million Words" after Gene agreed. This is how it concluded:

So I go in for my last words, because I have to go back home, and my mother and I agree I probably won't see him again. I sit next to him on the bed, hoping he can't see that I'm crying. "I love you, Dad," I say. He says: "I love you, too. I'd like some oatmeal."

So I go back out to the living room, where my mother and my wife and my son are sitting on the sofa, in a line, waiting for the outcome. And I say, "He wants some oatmeal." I am laughing and crying about this. My mother thinks maybe I should go back in and try to have a more meaningful last talk, but I don't.

Driving home, I'm glad I didn't. I think: He and I have been talking ever since I learned how. A million words. All of them final, now. I don't need to make him give me any more, like souvenirs. I think: Let me not define his death on my terms. Let him have his oatmeal. I can hardly see the road.

Both of the memorial services we held for Dad—one in Armonk and one in New York City—were packed with people and tears. He was adored by so many. Only Mom, Kate, Phil, Sam, and I went to the small rural cemetery to bury his ashes, which were in a cardboard box, following the Armonk service. We placed the box in the hole that had been dug by the cemetery workers. We cried, hugged, and exchanged a few words.

After that, we left the hole. We were still crying, and it was pouring. Mom was reading the names on the surrounding gravestones while she held my arm. She abruptly stopped.

She cried out, "So that's why we don't see him around anymore." At this point, we were all crying and laughing.

Dad would have been laughing the hardest.

Mom was humorous even at that time, just after she had buried her 42-year-married husband. She had a knack for humor.

However, humorous does not equal happiness.

Mom had long suffered from depression, a dark, hopeless state of mind that would sometimes last for days at a time. She took prescription antidepressants and saw psychiatrists for years, but the darkness persisted. She frequently discussed suicide, which she unreservedly believed to be her right.

We were aware of Mom's mood swings as children, but she was typically able to handle them by carrying out her responsibilities as a mother and making a concerted effort to keep her issues from becoming our problems. She was able to control her depression, or at least cope with it, for the most part over the years.

Then Dad passed away. She had suffered during his years of drunkenness, so he hadn't been a model husband. However, for most of their marriage, he provided her stability and support. He got her because he loved her. She lost her anchor when she lost him. She wasn't certain of her career goals or where she wanted to reside. She will ultimately figure it out and find her way to a new life, I guess we all assumed. She was still healthy and had friends.

She also retained her sense of humor. After Dad passed away, she briefly worked for Joe DiGiacinto, a lawyer with a White Plains, New York, practice, as a secretary and legal assistant. Joe is my closest and oldest friend from Armonk; we went to school together from kindergarten through high school and were born at Mount Kisco Hospital only a few days apart. Although we can never get Joe to bill us, he has become the unofficial legal counsel for the Barry family throughout the years and knows my family very well. Because my mom was intelligent, a skilled typist, and a very pleasant person to deal with, he was glad to hire her and adored her. Her letters were excellent. Joe once handled a small legal matter concerning my newspaper column when she was employed by him.

She wrote it over two years after Dad passed away, and at that time, she seemed to be doing well, at least to me.

However, she wasn't.

Perhaps it was time to leave Armonk, so she decided to sell the house. However, she was unsure about her destination. She spent a few months around the nation, briefly residing in Florida with me and in California with my brothers, Sam and Phil. However, she was unable to find what she was seeking for and couldn't decide on a location. She had expressed interest in moving to Connecticut, so I took a plane up from Florida to show her around. I wrote an essay on that trip called "Lost in America" a few months later. Here it is:

My mother and I are driving through Hartford, Conn., on the way to a town called Essex. Neither of us has ever been to Essex, but we're both desperately hoping that my mother will want to live there.

She has been rootless for several months now, moving from son to son around the country, ever since she sold the house she had lived in for 40 years, the house she raised us in, the house my father built. Home where he died, April 4, 1984. She would note the date each year on the calendar in the kitchen.

"Dave died, 1984," the note would say. "Come back, Dave."

The note for July 5, their anniversary, said: "Married Dave, 1942. Best thing that ever happened to me."

The house was too big for my mother to handle alone, and we all advised her to sell it. Finally she did, and she shipped all her furniture to Sunnyvale, Calif., where my brother Phil lived. Her plan was to stay with him until she found her own place there.

Only she hated Sunnyvale. At first this seemed almost funny, even to her. "All my worldly goods," she would say, marveling at it, "are in a warehouse in Sunnyvale, Calif., which I hate." She always had a wonderful sense of absurdity.

After a while it didn't seem so funny. My mother left Sunnyvale to live for a while with my brother Sam, in San Francisco, and then with me, in Florida; but she didn't want to stay with us. What she wanted was a home.

What she really wanted was her old house.

With my father in it.

Of course she knew she couldn't have that, but when she tried to think of what else she wanted, her mind would just lock up. She started spending a lot of time watching soap operas.

"You have to get on with your life," I would tell her, in this new, parental voice I was developing when I talked to her. Dutifully, she

16

would turn off the TV and get out a map of the United States, which I bought her to help her think.

"Maybe Boulder would be nice," she would say, looking at Colorado. "I was born near Boulder."

"Mom," I would say in my new voice. "We've talked about Boulder 50 times, and you always end up saying you don't really want to live there."

Chastened, she would look back at her map, but I could tell she wasn't really seeing it.

"You have to be realistic," I would say. The voice of wisdom.

When she and I had driven each other just about crazy, she went back out to California, and repeated the process with both of my brothers. Then one night she called to ask, very apologetically, if I would go with her to look at Essex, Conn., which she had heard was nice. It was a bad time for me, but of course I said yes, because your mom is your mom. I met her in Hartford and rented a car.

I'm driving; my mother is looking out the window.

"I came through Hartford last year with Frank and Mil, on the way to Maine," she says. Frank was my father's brother; he has just died. My mother loved to see him. He reminded her of my father.

"We were singing," my mother says. She starts to sing.

I'm forever blowing bubbles

Pretty bubbles in the air.

I can tell she wants me to sing, too. I know the words; we sang this song when I was little.

First they fly so high, nearly reach the sky

Then like my dreams, they fade and die.

But I don't sing. I am all business.

"I miss Frank," says my mother.

Essex is a beautiful little town. We look at two nice, affordable apartments. But I can tell right away that my mother doesn't want to be there. She doesn't want to say so, after asking me to fly up from Miami, but we both know.

The next morning, in the motel coffee shop, we have a very tense breakfast.

"Look, Mom," I say, "you have to make some kind of decision." Sounding very reasonable.

She looks down at her map. She starts talking about Boulder again. This sets me off. I lecture her, tell her she's being childish. She's looking down at her map, gripping it. I drive her back to Hartford, neither of us saying much. I put her on a plane; she's going to Milwaukee, to visit my dad's sister, then back to my brother in Sunnyvale, Calif. Which she hates.

The truth is, I'm relieved that she's leaving.

"You can't help her," I tell myself, "until she decides what she wants." It is a sound position.

About a week later, my wife and I get a card from my mother.

"This is to say happy birthday this very special year," it says. "And to thank you for everything."

Our birthdays are weeks away.

About two days later, my brother Phil calls, crying, from a hospital. My mother has taken a massive overdose of Valium and alcohol. Doctors want permission to shut machines. They say there's no hope. We talk about it, but there really isn't much to say. We give the permission.

It's the only logical choice.

The last thing I saw my mother do, just before she went down the tunnel to her plane, was turn and give me a big smile. It wasn't a smile of happiness; it was the same smile I give my son when he gets upset listening to the news, and I tell him don't worry, we're never going to have a nuclear war

I can still see that smile any time I want. Close my eyes, and there it is. A mom, trying to reassure her boy that everything's going to be OK.

That last meeting with Mom still makes me feel bad because I was so self-centered and naive to assume I understood what she needed to do when I had no idea what she was going through. She saw no other option to end the excruciating suffering she was experiencing.

Additionally, I believe she didn't want to cause her children to suffer through her suffering. I believe she saw her leaving our lives as an act of maternal love.

I didn't anticipate it, I didn't realize how much she was going through, and I didn't take any significant action to assist her. I got her a dumb map instead. And that guilt will always be a part of me.

However, thankfulness rather than guilt is the main emotion that comes to mind when I think about my mother. I owe a lot of my personality and my entire career to her; she was the funniest and sharpest person I ever met. Just as I wouldn't minimize my dad's life to a battle with drinking, I wouldn't minimize hers to a battle with depression. Despite not being Ozzie and Harriet, they were both nice people—smart, humorous, and decent—and they made great role models and parents. They provided us Barry children with a lovely upbringing and taught us how to behave by modeling it for others. It was mostly your traditional, traditional Midwestern values:

Refrain from acting superior to others. Treat everyone with courtesy, not just those you want to win.

Don't brag about yourself; be humble. People will understand what makes you unique.

Never take anything too seriously, especially. Not you in particular.

I still make an effort to live up to these admirable ideals. And I've made a feeble attempt to teach them to my own children. The older I get, the more I realize that my parents' wisdom is the most valuable thing I possess.

Thank you, Dad and Mom.

CHAPTER 2
SCHOOL

I started my education at Wampus Elementary, a public school that continues to educate Armonk's youngsters. ("Wampus" is derived from the Native American word "wampus," which means, to the best of my knowledge, "Wampus."

In 1952, I began kindergarten. We were deep in the Cold War with the Russians, the nuclear arms race was underway, and Harry Truman was president. The first hydrogen bomb was tested in the United States shortly after the 1952 school year. It was such a huge event that we even heard about it on the playground at Wampus Elementary. I recall older children, more enthusiastic than afraid, rushing around yelling, "H-bomb!"

The famed "duck and cover" drills, in which we kids would practice crawling beneath our desks to defend ourselves in the case of a nuclear bomb, were one of the most notable examples of how atomic war was taught in schools in the 1950s. We actually did that. At the time, when the possibility of a nuclear strike seemed very real, it also looked quite foolish. I believe we all secretly understood that school desks offered no real defense against atomic bombs; if they did, why not place enormous school desks over the main cities? The duck-and-cover exercises, however, didn't bother us at all. For instance, they were more entertaining than school.

Some individuals constructed fallout shelters, which were popular in the 1950s and early 1960s. There was no one I knew with one. My dad had a lot of work just giving us a normal place to live, so my family didn't.

I did, however, have a survival kit for a short time. In theory, this was a set of supplies that would let you survive a nuclear conflict. Although I can't recall where I got the idea, I do recall, at the age of ten or eleven, packing a lot of stuff into one of my dad's old toolboxes and carrying it around. (I also recall that my mother thought this was funny.) I think

I had a penknife, matches, and a flashlight in my survival kit. I do remember, however, two Hershey bars, which I evidently believed would give me essential nutrition amid the radioactive hellscape that Armonk would be reduced to after a nuclear missile exchange with the Russians.

As it happened, the Russians were unable to strike Armonk, and we may never know if this was because I had put together a survival bag. I ate the Hershey bars—they were just lying there, wasting away—after a day or two of carrying my toolbox around, and that was pretty much the end of my organized survival efforts.

The second terrifying memory I have of my early school years is of polio, or poliomyelitis, a highly contagious and incurable disease that afflicted children and had the potential to paralyze and kill them. In the early 1950s, there was a polio outbreak, and adults were afraid. Although our parents made an effort to conceal their anxieties from us, we could hear them discussing them—about families they knew had been affected, and about what they needed to do to keep us safe. They were concerned about if and where we could play, whether our playmates would get colds, and they were quite concerned about us getting colds. Although we were young, we could sense their concern. Then, in 1952, Dr. Jonas Salk developed a polio-prevention vaccine. The good news was that. The way this vaccine was given was the bad news—for me, it was really horrible news.

A shot.

I was in first grade when all of the pupils at Wampus Elementary were lined up on the playground on a lovely, sunny May day in 1954. Dr. Mortimer "Monty" Cohn was waiting with a harpoon-sized needle as we were led one by one into the cafeteria. That is how it appeared to me.

Needles are something I detest. I have detested them throughout my life; I have ended myself asleep on the floor of multiple medical facilities after receiving a shot or having a blood sample taken. My experience on that May day at Wampus Elementary playground—standing in that long line, taking one grim step at a time toward a fate that I considered to be WAY worse than either polio or death—will always be a large wad of scar tissue in the Bad Memories lobe of my brain, even though I am incredibly grateful to Dr. Salk for developing the vaccine and Dr. Cohn for administering it to me.

Polio vaccinations made national headlines. The vaccines at Wampus Elementary were the subject of an article published May 6, 1954, in the North Castle Villager, an Armonk-based newspaper. The headline says:

"A Lark," Say Kids, as Polio Shots Begin"

I assume the author of that headline is no longer with us, but if they are still alive and chance to be reading this, allow me to respectfully say to them: YOU ARE A LYING LIAR. No one believed it was "a lark," even though maybe not all of the kids receiving shots that day were as large as I was. Furthermore, none of us—I'm speaking for my generation here—would have ever used the word "lark," even if we had liked it.

This is how the Villager article starts:

Hesitation gave way to curiosity and then to pride this week as hundreds of Northern Westchester school children found there's really nothing to taking the Salk anti-polio shots.

A few lips may have quivered at first, and there was a little doubt here and there as to just what the needle would feel like. But afterward it was all smiles.

Again, with all due respect: IT WAS NOT "ALL SMILES," YOU LYING NEWSPAPER LIAR WHO CLEARLY WAS NOT THERE. The Villager article continues:

The second round of shots will be given next week, and the final set four weeks later.

Half the children receive the vaccine, the other half a harmless control fluid. Study after the polio season will show the effectiveness of the vaccine. Only children in grades one through three are receiving the shots.

The names of the students who received the vaccination were printed in the Villager nearly a year later. Several of my classmates' names were among them, as was my sister's. However, my name was absent. I needed extra shots because I had been administered the "harmless control fluid." Compared to my sister, I need twice as many vaccinations.

This, I believe, explains why I became an atheist in the first place.

Anyway, primary school was a decent experience, except for polio and nuclear Armageddon. I gained useful abilities like reading and writing, which I occasionally use now. My first reading materials were the well-known Dick and Jane series, which featured two innocent-looking kids who had a nervous tic that made them talk like performers in a pornographic film's climax:

Dick said, "Oh, Jane. Oh, oh, oh."
Jane said, "Yes, Dick. Yes, yes, yes."
Dick said, "Ohmigod, Jane."

Additionally, I learned how to add and subtract, which ended up being the only math abilities I have ever truly needed in my adult life (although I must admit that I haven't done much subtraction). Using construction paper and this white paste (you Boomers remember this paste), I created art projects that ended up tasting really good. The food served in the cafeteria at Wampus Elementary, which was made from enormous government cans leftover from a previous conflict—possibly the French and Indian—was far less enjoyable to me than that paste.

Recess, when we children were let out into the playground to play Davy Crockett, chase each other, toss objects, and swing on the swings and slides, was the highlight of elementary school. The first significant fad I can recall was that one. Rifle-wielding, bear-shooting, coonskin-cap-wearing, Alamo-dying, franchise-anchoring, frontiersman Davy Crockett was the focus of a 1954 miniseries on Walt Disney's Disneyland television program. Everybody who watched that show was familiar with the Davy Crockett song:

Davy, Davy Crockett
King of the wild frontier!

Whenever I could, I wore my Davy Crockett T-shirt. We boys performed out the scene from the TV show's finale episode, in which Davy Crockett makes his valiant last stand and repels the Mexican attackers at the Alamo, on the playground at Wampus Elementary during recess. (The episode ends with actor Fess Parker, who has run out of bullets, swinging his rifle at the Mexicans, resembling a man practicing with a nine iron.) Disney did not show him actually dying.

A large boulder with a flat top that allowed you to stand on it served as the Alamo in our playground reenactment. Everyone wanted to play Davy Crockett, which was the issue. Since I had both the name and the T-shirt, I definitely did. No one desired to be Mexican. In essence, our reenactment had a group of young boys standing on a rock and attempting to appear brave in the face of an invisible Mexican horde that was on the attack.

To avoid becoming mired in a Boomer nostalgia for 1950s television (Howdy Doody! Lassie! Winky Dink!) When I was in fifth grade, I went to Whippoorwill School, a grand red-brick edifice from 1924 that was once Armonk's lone public school. Today, it's a condominium complex where, according to Zillow, a two-bedroom apartment costs over $700,000. The idea that individuals have spent that much to live in places where my classmates and I used to sit at awkward tables covered in graffiti and stare at mimeographed test pages in Mrs. DeLucia's class, frantically attempting to recall Vermont's capital, makes me laugh.

The Important News Sputnik was an event that occurred when I was in fifth grade. The Russians launched the world's first artificial satellite into orbit in October 1957, and boy, did it ever annoy the adults. We Americans simply believed we were technologically superior to the Russians until Sputnik. Why not? Our vehicles were better! We had way more TV! Color TV was even available to certain Americans! Of course, the color rendering was awful, so everyone on TV looked like they had deadly skin conditions. Still, though! Not even color television was available to the Russians! Consequently, how were they able to send up a functional satellite before we did?

Indeed, Sputnik did serious damage to American pride. However, we are not a quitter nation. The United States of America did not give up on the Space Race, just as Davy Crockett did not stop beating Mexicans at the Alamo until he was dead. A group of American scientists, engineers, military personnel, and civilian leaders assembled in Cape Canaveral on December 6, 1957, less than two months after the Sputnik launch, to witness the launch of the country's first satellite. This is how it was described on Wikipedia:

The booster ignited and began to rise. About two seconds after liftoff, after rising about 1.2 m (four feet), the rocket lost thrust and fell back to the launch pad. As it settled, the fuel tanks ruptured and exploded, destroying the rocket and severely damaging the launch pad. The Vanguard 1A satellite was thrown clear and landed on the ground a short distance away with its transmitters still sending out a beacon signal.

That's correct: Our rocket flew to about the height of a mailbox before exploding, whereas Sputnik was hundreds of miles above us, speeding at eighteen thousand miles per hour, and emitting happy futuristic beeps as it buzzed around the Earth once every ninety-six minutes. On the bright side, our satellite bravely kept sending out beacon signals, which made it simple to find while it lay on the ground.

Thus, the United States suddenly lost its sense of superiority. As I mentioned before, this completely frightened out the adults of 1957. Someone had totally failed; something had gone horribly wrong. Our nation's leaders believed it was time to assign the blame to the fifth graders at Whippoorwill School, where it belonged.

That's how it felt, anyway. All of a sudden, we students heard a lot from our instructors, who in turn heard it from the politicians, about how America's youth needed to get better at science and math. We were going to get more math and science lessons, we were going to get more homework, and we were supposed to understand algebra and trigonometry, including something called the "cosine," which none of us—I speak for my generation here—have ever truly understood the purpose of. It didn't matter that the Russians were winning the Space

Race; we were the ones who were supposed to understand it. Did the leaders of our country, who were in command when we lost the Space Race, have to deal with the task of figuring out the "cosine"? No, they didn't. They gave the fifth graders at Whippoorwill School that unachievable assignment.

We're still resentful, as you can see.

Following Whippoorwill, I went to Harold C. Crittenden Junior High School, which is still educating Armonk's youngsters today as H. C. Crittenden Middle School, grades six to nine. For me, junior high was an exciting time—by which I mean "deeply disturbing." This was due to an incident I had there that I would not want to happen to anybody else and that I am still hesitant to discuss.

adolescence.

The length of time it took for puberty to come was the worst thing about it for me. I developed late. I was stuck with a little larger version of the tiny hairless body I'd been flaunting since my Davy Crockett days, as one by one of my male classmates began to grow taller, talk in a deeper voice, and sprout hair in new places.

And my male classmates weren't the only ones who were evolving. When we got back from summer vacation at the start of seventh grade, it was clear that the girls were changing even more dramatically. The girls had changed from being girls to young women. They all seemed to have gone to Summer Bosom Camp. In the form of semipermanent boners, the guys were undoubtedly aware of this and experiencing strong new biological stirrings. Harold C. Crittenden Junior High was experiencing a Category 5 puberty storm, with hormone waves sloshing through the hallways.

Additionally, our social lives were evolving. We stopped hosting parties with cake, ice cream, balloons, and pin the tail on the donkey under the supervision of adults. Rather, we were enjoying adult-free gatherings where we would spin bottles, slow dance, hold hands, kiss, make out, and occasionally, rumor has it, reach bases. In class, we were exchanging notes. We had dates planned. We were moving steadily.

I was still waiting for the Puberty Fairy to come visit. My dad chopped my hair with electric clippers he purchased from a pharmacy, and I wore heavy glasses. My father was a really good man, as I have already shown, but he was neither a professional barber nor a professional home builder. He trimmed all of my hair to the same length—short—quickly and effectively, much like someone would mow a lawn. I ended up with a hairstyle that left me with a naked forehead that looked like it was the size of a proper volleyball court.

I therefore did not belong to the Cute Boys. The girls didn't like me. In eighth grade, I did try one serious date, and it was so incredibly awkward that, even after thirty-two years, I could still clearly recall it enough to write a column about it. I'll quote the piece here because, despite its comic intent, it's actually pretty accurate:

The first dating rule is: Never risk direct contact with the girl in question. Your role model should be the nuclear submarine, gliding silently beneath the ocean surface, tracking an enemy target that does not even begin to suspect that the submarine would like to date it. I spent the vast majority of 1960 keeping a girl named Judy under surveillance, maintaining a minimum distance of 50 lockers to avoid the danger that I might somehow get into a conversation with her, which could have led to disaster:

Judy: Hi.

Me: Hi.

Judy: Just in case you have ever thought about having a date with me, the answer is no.

The only problem with the nuclear-submarine technique is that it's difficult to get a date with a girl who has never, technically, been asked. This is why you need Phil Grant. Phil was my friend who had the ability to talk to girls. It was a mysterious superhuman power he had, comparable to X-ray vision.

So, after several thousand hours of intense discussion and planning with me, Phil approached a girl he knew named Nancy, who approached a girl named Sandy, who was a direct personal friend of Judy's and who passed the word back to Phil via Nancy that Judy would be willing to go on a date with me. This procedure protected me from direct humiliation, similar to the way President Reagan was protected from direct involvement in the Iran-contra scandal by a complex White House chain of command that at one point, investigators now believe, included his horse.

Thus it was that, finally, Judy and I went on an actual date, to see a movie in White Plains, New York. If I were to sum up the romantic ambience of this date in four words, those words would be: "My mother was driving." This made for an extremely quiet drive, because my mother, realizing that her presence was hideously embarrassing, had to pretend she wasn't there. If it had been legal, I think she would have got out and sprinted alongside the car, steering through the window.

Judy and I, sitting in the back seat about 75 feet apart, were also silent, unable to communicate without the assistance of Phil, Nancy and Sandy. After what seemed like several years we got to the movie theater, where my mother went off to sit in the Parents and Lepers Section.

The movie was called North to Alaska, but I can tell you nothing else about it because I spent the whole time wondering whether it would be necessary to amputate my right arm, which was not getting any blood flow as a result of being perched for two hours like a petrified snake on the back of Judy's seat exactly one molecule away from physical contact. So it was definitely a fun first date, featuring all the relaxed spontaneity of a real-estate closing, and in later years I did regain some feeling in my arm.

Other than that extremely painful experience, I had little one-on-one interaction with girls in junior high. At parties, when other boys were slow-dancing with girls and attempting to reach bases in dark corners, I was the person operating the record player and amusing the other puberty-impaired loser boys by making hand farts. This was the genesis of my career in humor.

The big organized youth social event in Armonk back then was Canteen, which was held on Friday nights at Crittenden Junior High.

I believe the idea was to give us youths a wholesome, supervised activity so that we wouldn't spend the weekend nights committing acts of vandalism. And it worked! At least it worked on Friday nights. There was still vandalism on Saturday nights.

There were two main elements to Canteen: the gym, where the boys played basketball, and the cafeteria, where the girls danced to 45 r.p.m. records with each other until the gym was closed, at which point the boys went to the cafeteria and either danced with girls or (this was me) stood around wishing they had the confidence to dance with girls.

One record that got a lot of play in the Crittenden cafeteria, and on the planet in general, was "The Twist." This was the Chubby Checker song that was a huge success, reaching number one in 1960 and again in 1962 and inspiring a monster dance craze. Why was the Twist so popular? The answer is simple: White people could do it. Anybody could do it. Our parents could do it. It was an easily replicated mechanical movement requiring no natural dancing ability whatsoever to execute. Even I sometimes did the Twist. I still do the Twist, at weddings. That is the impact it had on me.

Aside from the Twist, the other major world event I remember from my junior-high years is the presidential election of 1960, John F. Kennedy vs. Richard M. Nixon. This was the first election I paid attention to. It was a big deal for my parents, who were still sad about the fact that in the 1952 and 1956 elections, their candidate, Adlai Stevenson, had lost to Dwight Eisenhower, because the American people were simply not ready—will probably never be ready—for a president named "Adlai."

My parents had strong Democratic views. However, they had good pals who shared their fervent Republican views. At cocktail gatherings, I recall listening to them quarrel over politics. Cocktail parties were popular back then. People would frequently dress up and go to each other's homes to smoke cigarettes, drink alcohol, sing, dance, and generally have a good time without feeling guilty about it. Almost every weekend in Armonk, my parents threw or attended cocktail parties. Our house would be packed with people and commotion while they were hosting. As Barry kids, we found this to be really thrilling and would listen in on the celebrations. We heard some intense, emotive, and occasionally irate exchanges between Republicans and Democrats during the Kennedy-Nixon campaign. Never nasty, though. Because they were friends and realized that they could disagree on politics without considering the opposing viewpoint to be malevolent, everyone gave each other hugs at the end of the evening. Perhaps I was wrong. No, evil.

The 1960s Armonk adults had their shortcomings. They smoked foolishly, drank too much, and looked stupid when they performed the Twist. However, they were far more sensible than we are now when it comes to politics. They realized that the majority of people share a common set of goals, including justice, peace, and a good life for themselves and their children, and that politics is essentially a debate over the best ways to get there. Therefore, they did not automatically think that everybody who disagreed with them was a jerk, which is essentially how we currently do politics.

The dynamic between teachers and students was another aspect that was different in those days. The disciplinary methods my junior-high teachers frequently employed would likely land them in jail today. For instance, Mr. Schofield, our arithmetic instructor, had great aim and would hurl chalk at you if you weren't paying attention. Mr. Friedman, a social studies teacher who was a little less precise threw erasers. Mr. Fletcher, a history teacher, would use his hand, which felt like it weighed eleven pounds, to strike you in the head if you were a wayward or inattentive boy (girls were excluded from this). Some of us still bear the scars from Mr. Fletcher's lesson on our skulls.

We didn't think these disciplinary actions were odd or harsh. Telling our parents that a teacher had hit us or thrown something at us would never have occurred to us; if we had, they would have questioned us about what we had done wrong to merit it. I'm not advocating for physical punishment as the best method of student discipline. In the classes taught by Mr. Friedman, Mr. Schofield, and most importantly, Mr. Fletcher, we had a tendency to pay attention.

The sex-based curriculum was another element of our Harold C. Crittenden education that would not work in the modern world: Girls studied home economics, and boys studied shop. No choices, no exclusions. We boys would go to the shop at specific times of the week to learn, over the course of several months, how to use tools to transform pieces of wood into slightly smaller, brown-stained pieces. When we men returned from our breadwinner professions manufacturing brown-stained wooden objects, the girls were in the home ec room, wearing aprons and baking cookies in preparation for future occupations in which they would stay at home, raise the children, and bake food for us to eat.

As it happened, the majority of the females went on to have employment outside the home. Most of us never used our carpentry expertise. Glenn Close, a longtime student at Harold C. Crittenden Junior High, was one of the girls who did. Actually. I will never forget a discussion I had with her one morning while we were waiting for school to start. She was in my eighth grade homeroom.

I urged her to forget cookies. "You ought to become a well-known actress."

No, I'm joking. Even though Glenn Close was in my homeroom, I don't remember any of the conversations we had. She was pleasant, I remember that.

Since public schools in Armonk only offered ninth grade in 1962, my class at Pleasantville High School, a few miles away, began tenth grade that year. As the name implies, Pleasantville was a pleasant, all-American community; in fact, Reader's Digest was based there. Pleasantville High, a large red-brick structure with a traditional white-columned portico outside, nevertheless had the appearance of a high school from a motion picture.

The majority of the student population entered by that portico, so we went under the careful eye of Anthony Sabella, the assistant principle. He was a big, stocky man who was widely known as Tough Tony, though no one addressed him by that name. Every morning, Mr. Sabella, who also served as a high school sports referee, waited by the front door to check entering pupils for dress code infractions. He seemed to know everyone's name, so if he noticed a female with an excessively short skirt, a boy with too long hair, or a boy wearing too tight pants (thin white Levi's were a hot look), he would yell the student's name and send them home to fix the issue.

Throughout the school day, Mr. Sabella patrolled the hallways in the manner of a referee, searching for infractions. If he saw you committing one, he would not hesitate to take you by the neck—I can attest to this—and tell you that your punishment was typically detention. The principal, Mr. McCreary, a little, gray, formal man who had served as principal from the beginning of time, was officially the top authority at Pleasantville High. However, Tough Tony was the man in charge of the school.

Although I ultimately enjoyed my time at Pleasantville, I was initially very intimidated—and not just by Mr. Sabella. Many of the kids seemed incredibly old to me, like real adults with automobiles, and I didn't know most of them. The cliques, the cheerleaders, the jocks, the nerds, the student-government go-getters, the arty kids, the hoods, and the tough girls with enormous beehive hairstyles that, according to urban legend, had been firmly hair-sprayed in place for so long that they held spider colonies were all part of the hierarchy, which was present in every high school. On Friday, there were pep rallies for the Pleasantville football team, and on Saturday, the majority of the school attended the games. There was an alma mater, clubs, groups, dances, and customs. For a while, I didn't feel like I belonged to any of Pleasantville High's many intricate social groups.

However, I eventually discovered my specialty and my high school persona, which was essentially wiseass, as everyone does. Lanny Watts, a highly intelligent and humorous man I met in tenth school who became my best friend and accomplice in many of my foolish deeds, joined me in this role.

Lanny and I took great satisfaction in making fun of everything and not taking anything seriously. Our goal in life was to ridicule. As an illustration: We became members of the fencing club at Pleasantville

High. We simply found the concept of the fencing club amusing; we had no interest in competitive fencing at all.

After the initial meeting, none of our club members remained. The club's faculty adviser, who I believe was a French instructor, gave the fencers some rudimentary instruction before we practiced lunging at one another in pairs. I wrote a column about what transpired after many years:

Lanny was paired against one of the veteran club members, who had assumed his fighting stance, holding his fencing sword in the ready position. Suddenly Lanny ran from the room, only to return a moment later holding: a trombone. Even though I was lying on the floor and trying not to wet my pants, I still have a vivid motion picture in my mind of the scene that followed: Lanny charging forward, blowing into the trombone and thrusting boldly with the sliding part, as his opponent retreated in confusion and—yes—fear. Lanny and I were immediately kicked out of the fencing club. But I think they knew who won.

That is still one of my favorite memories from high school. But wasn't it kind of annoying, you might be thinking? When the other students were taking fencing seriously, were you interfering with their practice?

Yes, it was annoying, is the response. As an old person looking back, I acknowledge that Lanny and I were sometimes total jerks, and I apologize to any former Pleasantville High fencing club members who may be reading this. We made a mistake.

Nevertheless: a trombone.

Lanny and I offered to serve on the publicity committee for the school's large dance when we were seniors. In fact, we were the committee as a whole. We obviously didn't volunteer because we genuinely wanted to promote the dance. We thought we had a great idea for adding a pornographic allusion to the dance posters, so we offered to help. Being seniors in the class of 1965 was crucial to this strategy. Thus, we created a number of posters that read:

WHEN YOU'RE IN THE COLLEGE CLASS OF

69
YOU'LL STILL REMEMBER THIS DANCE

Everything else was substantially smaller than the "69." Each poster was essentially a huge "69" with some text surrounding it. As I say, this struck Lanny and me as brilliant. The problem was, school administrators had to approve each poster. We decided that Principal McCreary was our best chance, so Lanny and I found him in the hallway outside his office one morning before school and gave him our posters. He stated they were fine after reading them, and to his credit, he was about 285 years old. Taking out his pen, he was about to initial the posters to show his approval when Mr. Sabella appeared. Oh no.

After glancing with the posters, Mr. Sabella, who was far more streetwise than Mr. McCreary, said they were unsuitable. "Because they have obscene implications," Mr. Sabella remarked, gazing at Lanny and me in response to Mr. McCreary's question. "Oh," murmured Mr. McCreary, flushed and confused. Our wonderful plan came to an end when Mr. Sabella gave Lanny and I instructions to shove our posters into a garbage can.

We were amazingly spared detention for the episode. I believe Mr. Sabella thought our actions were pranks rather than a major rule infraction. He was a sensible man, as scary as he might be. When I had him as a teacher, I discovered that he was even capable of being humorous. He was an assistant principal and one of my favorite high school teachers. He also taught American history. He promoted free-flowing conversation and was an interesting speaker. He actually enjoyed it when you argued with him, so it didn't bother him. Given how many times he essentially carried me off the ground by my neck, it's funny that Mr. Sabella ended up being one of the Pleasantville residents I remember the most.

Regina Adams, who taught English composition, is another educator I have pleasant memories of. In her class, we wrote many essays. I eventually tried to make mine humorous, and she supported me. She loved one of my essays so much that she asked me to read it aloud to the class. It was about how eager she was for the school year to end. My carefully crafted image was wiseass, not teacher's pet, so I most definitely did not want to do that. Mrs. Adams requested permission to read the essay aloud to the class while identifying the author. That was fine with me. My classmates laughed appropriately when Mrs. Adams read my article. Hearing others chuckle at what I had to say felt fantastic. It continues to do so. I'm grateful, Mrs. Adams.

The school newspaper, the Green Lantern (the colors of Pleasantville were green and white), published my first funny essay in my senior year. My friend Tom Parker served as coeditor so that he could write "Editor of School Newspaper" on his Yale application, not because he was interested in journalism. Philomène Dursin, the other coeditor, carried out the real work in accordance with the long-standing tradition of women working in organizations alongside men.

However, as I mentioned before, Tom was a buddy of mine, so I wrote an article for the Green Lantern about the senior boys' loadball game, which is an unofficial Pleasantville tradition. Boys in their final year played a game of tackle football on a muddy field while drinking a lot of alcohol. There were no rules, and no one kept score. At any given time, forty or fifty players may be participating, and occasionally more than one football. It was violent, disorderly, and incredibly foolish. I had a great time.

It is understood the school did not approve the loadball match. Naturally, I wanted to get it into the school newspaper because they would never cover it for whatever reason. I accomplished this by writing about it as though it were a real sporting event, mentioning beer in passing but not explicitly. The only joke I can think of is about players with cut thumbs being sidelined, but I don't have the original piece. I can't recall if my classmates found my anecdote amusing or not. However, I do recall finding it enjoyable to see in paper.

As previously stated, I ended up enjoying high school, which was primarily a stress-free and enjoyable experience for me, notwithstanding the occasional zit. I lived in a cozy little world.

Though it didn't really impact me, I was dimly aware that there was a wider world outside of Armonk and Pleasantville.

But it was beginning to change. The cozy mediocrity of the 1950s had subsided, and the sixties, in all its forms—good, bad, and strange— were about to pierce my tiny cocoon.

The March on Washington on August 28, 1963, where Martin Luther King delivered his "I Have a Dream" speech, was my first real experience of the 1960s, and it was unquestionably positive. I was present. Along with several Camp Sharparoon employees, I took a bus down from New York City.

My dad's organization, the New York City Mission Society, ran two summer camps for inner-city children: Sharparoon and Camp Minisink. Going from Armonk, where everyone was white, to places where we were a racial minority was an eye-opening experience for us Barry kids who grew up as campers at both of these camps. I think my sister, Kate, and I were the only white campers at Camp Minisink during a few summers. I made friends, had a great time, picked up a lot of new lingo, and never once felt less than totally accepted by the other kids throughout those wonderful summers. In Armonk at the time, I sincerely doubt that a Black child would have been welcomed in the same manner.

Regardless, I was too old to camp by 1963, so I spent that summer working at Camp Sharparoon as a member of the maintenance team. Staff members who wished to attend the March on Washington, who were primarily college students, were given a trip by the City Mission Society at the end of the summer. We all joined hands, dressed in black and white, and sang "We Shall Overcome" during a large candlelight rally in Harlem the night before the march. which we genuinely thought we would.

We boarded busses early the following day and traveled to Washington, DC, where we joined the biggest gathering I had ever been a part of—hundreds of thousands of people—who were all hot, joyful, and full of hope. To hear the speeches, we assembled around the reflecting pool in front of the Lincoln Memorial. The speakers' stage was around a hundred yards away from me. My parents were closer; one of the speakers that day was my buddy Whitney Young Jr., the leader of the Urban League, who was hosting Dad.

Dr. King was the star, and we couldn't wait to hear him speak. However, I doubt that most of us—at least not me—realized how well-known that specch would become. I primarily recall the sense of belonging to something very significant and being positive. As the years passed, the sixties faded, and I grew older, I would have this feeling less frequently.

The Dallas gut punch came just under three months after the March on Washington's euphoria. I was in Spanish class at Pleasantville High. Miss Nauman, the instructor, came late, sobbing, and informed us that President Kennedy had been shot. There was clearly going to be no Spanish that day, and we all sat there in disbelief. Another instructor stepped in minutes later to tell us that the president was reportedly dead, according to the TV news.

It was canceled; school ended early. On what was known as the Corner, where kids frequently congregated to smoke, joke around, and generally act like teenagers when they band together, I was among the milling mob of students waiting for our buses across from the high school.

That day, however, we were a quiet group. For the first time in my memory, I felt the unpleasant feeling that would become commonplace in my sixties: that big things were happening, that no one had anticipated, that no one really understood. Up until Dallas, at least to me, it seemed like someone was in charge—someone significant, an elderly person in a suit, someone with all the necessary knowledge. After Dallas, it became increasingly apparent that no one was in charge. That played a significant role in the ambiance of the 1960s.

In the fall of 1963, I received a driver's license from the New York State Department of Motor Vehicles, which I do not intend to link to the Kennedy assassination, even though it was a significant event for me. In a state of pure automotive ecstasy, I jumped into my mom's car the day it arrived and drove it erratically across the greater Armonk area for at least a hundred miles.

The 1961 Plymouth Valiant station wagon that my mother was driving at the time was maybe the least interesting vehicle ever made—the soybean curd of automobiles. In about two weeks, it went from zero to sixty, and it was awful. In other words, it was a normal family vehicle owned by Barry. Despite never having much money, my dad always purchased used cars, but they were often not your typical used cars like Fords or Chevys. For good reason, most of them were mutant vehicles nobody else owned.

For instance, we had a British vehicle known as a Hillman Minx for a short but thrilling period of time. This was a black, boxy car with a technical flaw that occasionally, at least in ours, caused the steering wheel to abruptly separate from the front wheels. Actually. The Minx would continue traveling in the same direction even if you turned the steering wheel all the way around. The driver would stamp wildly on the brakes and, in my dad's case, use non-Presbyterian language. Since they were all pushed into the sea, I assume that there are no Minxes remaining in England.

The Nash Metropolitan, a little car with amusingly cartoonish design, came after the Minx. It appeared to be the protagonist of Carl the Car's Big Adventure, a comic book. Fortunately, the steering functioned. Unfortunately, the motor—which turns out to be a crucial part— frequently failed to function. The Metropolitan was far safer than the Minx as a result, but it wasn't as practical for traveling from point A to point B. It was better suited to standing still with the hood open at Point A.

Even though my mom's Plymouth Valiant was slow and ugly, it was a Ferrari in comparison to the Minx and the Metropolitan, and I took advantage of every opportunity to drive it after I obtained my driver's license. As Boomer suburban kids of the 1960s, we loved driving because it gave us the freedom to drive around unattended, pick up friends, honk at other kids, and listen to Top 40 music on the low-fidelity AM radio.

I gave in to the fast-talking, hepcat deejays of the major New York stations, such as Bruce "Cousin Brucie" Morrow on WABC and Murray the K and his Swingin' Soiree on WINS. Hits like the Angels' heartfelt, romantic ballad "My Boyfriend's Back," in which a young woman tells an unwelcome suitor that her real love has returned home and is going to beat the living daylights out of him, were played in late 1963. The Singing Nun, who sang "Dominique" in French with an annoyingly high-pitched voice, was the country's number-one song at the end of the year. The Kingsmen's number two single, "Louie Louie," was purportedly in English, but no one could understand the lyrics, so we thought they were filthy, which is one of the reasons we enjoyed them.

When 1964 dawned, we were listening to that music.

In January, we all seemed to hear it at once. It was an entirely new sound from England, beginning with those powerful chords that pushed you into the song: C to D, C to D, C to DEEEEEEEEE.

Indeed, I will tell you something.

The Beatles then burst onto the scene, playing on radios everywhere.

I can speak for my generation here when I say we fell in love with them right away, and not only for their music. We appreciated their humor, intelligence, and lack of self-importance. The fact that older people hated haircuts delighted us. We wanted to establish a band, grow our own hair long, and make screaming girls fall in love with us. At least I did, albeit the hair had to wait till Mr. Sabella stopped keeping an eye on my appearance.

In 1965, I received my diploma from Pleasantville. My classmates chose me Male Class Clown in appreciation of my contributions to the Class of '65's intellectual and cultural heritage. Additionally, I was selected to speak at the commencement, which was an honor I did not merit and completely did not take seriously. The details of what I said have thankfully slipped my mind, but I do recall that it was mostly meaningless nonsense about the Future, interspersed with a phrase from Bob Dylan about blowin' in the wind. I apologize to any of my classmates who could have been listening since I'm still ashamed of that speech.

The next step was college. I attended Haverford, a Quaker-founded tiny, all-male (now coed) institution in suburban Philadelphia. Although Haverford is a highly regarded academic institution, it is not well-known; I have long maintained that "We Never Heard of You, Either" ought to be its official motto.

Dave, Lanny Watts' older brother, attended Haverford, so I applied there. That was the only explanation. I chose to apply since it looked like a cool area when Lanny and I visited one weekend. If Haverford hadn't accepted me, I don't know what I would have done, so I didn't apply anywhere else. Although I now acknowledge that my attitude to this selection was excessively informal and almost foolish, selecting a college was not the crazy, never-ending, high-pressure affair that it is now, when parents begin to obsess over college while their unborn children are still in the womb.

Anyway, despite my initial fear of the other students, Haverford ended up being a fantastic place for me. I had always considered myself to be one of the smarter kids and had consistently had decent grades up to that point. However, everyone at Haverford had consistently received good marks, and they all appeared to be skilled in other ways, such as playing the French horn, hurling the javelin, becoming debate champs, chess experts, or thespians. The lecturers all appeared to be frighteningly smart, too.

I eventually found my way at Haverford, just as I did at Pleasantville High. I had a lot of noteworthy and occasionally quite entertaining events, and I made friends—really wonderful friends, guys who are still my friends now. Additionally, I received some education, though I must confess that this was not my top focus.

I read around one-third of many outstanding literary works because I was majoring in English. Technically, I was expected to finish reading these works, but due to my hectic schedule, I just did not have the opportunity to do so. The most of them, like The Brothers Karamazov, were quite lengthy.

Playing in rock bands took up a lot of my time at Haverford. Playing "Hang On Sloopy" for crowds of gyrating college students in widely disparate states of consciousness is what I remember most vividly from my four years at a top-tier university, where I was exposed to famous literature and eminent academic minds. I realize this may seem like a pitiful admission. Being in a band was my identity and true passion.

During my four years at Haverford, I participated in bands. In reality, it was a single band that used a variety of names and lineups. My first year we were known as the Stomp Jackson Quintet. There were five of us in the band, but I'm not positive because my memory is fuzzy. No one in the band was named Jackson. However, we thought the name was cool because, well, why not?

We then temporarily changed our name to the Guides in an attempt to seem hipper. We assumed the Guides would have a psychedelic moniker since we had heard that the word "guide" was a colloquial term for someone who assisted others in getting through LSD experiences. The problem was we were the only ones who had ever heard of this term. People were mispronouncing our name and assuming we were the Guys, which would have been a dumb band name (though not as dumb as the Guides, looking back).

We eventually came up with the moniker we utilized the most, the Federal Duck, sometime during my sophomore year. One evening while enjoying the evening air with a bunch of us sitting on the grassy bank of Haverford's picturesque little duck pond, a notion struck us. And I mean "smoking pot" when I say "enjoying the evening air."

We had been enjoying the evening air for a while when we saw that some ducks had come out of the pond and were waddling toward us. Bob Stern, my roommate, voiced fear that these ducks might be involved in a federal anti-drug operation as we watched them approach. Even though I believe he was kidding, we became worried when the ducks continued to arrive since (a) we were extremely inebriated and (b) those were separate times. Unlike today, when grandparents are doing edibles, marijuana is not only legal but also required in places like New York, based on the pot smell that permeates the air. Having a single joint back then might get you in serious difficulties, even jail time. We were hence prone to paranoia.

That's why we stood up and moved aside when the Haverford Pond ducks came closer. We knew our worries were unfounded, so we laughed. Ha ha! Obviously, we are not in danger from these ducks! They're ducks! However, we did relocate.

We also thought of a new name for the band. From that point on, we were known among our roughly three ardent supporters as the Federal Duck, or just the Duck. We performed frequently on some weekends on both Friday and Saturday nights since we were reasonably priced and dependable. Naturally, we performed at Haverford, but we also performed at fraternity parties and mixers at universities around the Philadelphia region, including Beaver, Villanova, Penn, Ursinus, Drexel, Temple, Harcum, and Bryn Mawr, our sister campus. We even played at Swarthmore, which was Haverford's fiercest opponent because both were Quaker-founded bookish colleges with poor athletic records.

We were a party band, not an arty band. We played a lot of simple bulletproof three-chord garage-band standards—songs like "Sloopy," "Louie Louie," "Gloria," "Money" and "Land of 1,000 Dances," which actually has only one chord and can go on for weeks if necessary. We played "Satisfaction," "Get Off of My Cloud" and "Under My Thumb" by the Stones, and "Purple Haze" by Jimi Hendrix. We played "96 Tears," by ? and the Mysterians. We played "Got My Mojo Working," the Butterfield Blues Band version, and "Knock on Wood," the James Cotton version. We played "I Can't Keep from Crying," the Blues Project version. We had no particular genre beyond Songs People Dance To. Sometimes we'd get requests, and we'd say, "Sure! We can do that!" Then we'd play "Land of 1,000 Dances."

Musically we were never anything special, though some of my bandmates were genuinely talented, particularly bassist Bob Stern and keyboardist Ken Stover, who both went on to play professionally. I was a ploddingly mediocre rhythm guitarist and singer. But as I say, we played a lot, and over time we became at least halfway decent.

We played in different conditions, not always hospitable. I remember playing an event for some college organization at a restaurant, and one of the waitresses—at the time I thought of her as an old lady, though she was probably in her thirties—stood directly in front of us for a few seconds, staring at us, then slowly, deliberately, raised her hands and stuck her forefingers into her ears. Not a fan of our sound.

We got used to playing through adversity. One time we played in a Penn frat house, in a room with a big window looking out onto the front porch. While we were performing there was a loud crash, and a sofa, which had been outside on the porch, came flying through the window into the room. The frat bros and their dates avoided the scattering glass, but they continued dancing; evidently this kind of occurrence was not that unusual. So we kept right on playing. As I recall the song was "Louie Louie."

Frat parties were the trickiest, especially when the brothers decided they wanted to grab our microphones and sing, or, worse, play our instruments. More than once I found myself wrestling with some drunk bro midsong for possession of my guitar. As the evening wore on, there occasionally were beer-fueled fights; sometimes there would be fighting, dancing and vomiting going on simultaneously. At some parties we'd line up our amps in front of us, forming a barrier for us to play behind. This was suboptimal from an acoustic standpoint, but we felt safer.

Notwithstanding the occasional hazardous gig, I loved being in the Federal Duck. The sixties were raging, and it was cool to be in a rock band, and I was in one. In the escalating culture war between old and young, squares and hippies, I was definitely on Team Hippie. I grew my hair long, which meant that when I left the Haverford campus, I was sometimes the target of anti-hippie remarks, especially when I happened to walk past groups of older men.

"Can't tell if that's a boy or a girl!" one of them would say—this was considered the height of wit—and the others would laugh, and depending on how likely it seemed that I might get the crap beat out of me, I'd either give them the finger or just keep walking.

I should note here that I did not spend my entire college career playing in a rock band and smoking pot. I also, time permitting, attended classes, and I wrote a lot of words. Many of these words were in the form of papers about great works of literature of which, as an English major, I had read roughly one-third. But some of the words were in the form of humor columns for the student newspaper, the Haverford News.

I began when I was given the task of writing a real news piece by the editor, Dennis Stern, a classmate of mine who later had a prestigious career at the New York Times. The job, if I remember right, was to cover the Nixon for President campaign in Ardmore, a town adjacent to Haverford. I stayed in my dorm room and wrote a humorous piece on the Nixon campaign's entrance since, as a long-haired, pot-smoking hippy, I had absolutely no desire to speak with any Nixon folks. Dennis may have published it, but I can't recall. However, he prudently employed me as a humor columnist rather than a reporter after that.

I may have contributed a dozen or so humorous columns to the Haverford News. When the Class of 1969 gathered in the Haverford gym for their thirtieth reunion years later, someone hung enlarged copies of some of my columns on the walls. Even though I thought they were amusing when I wrote them, the older me didn't find them so funny. The pot might have been the cause.

During my student years, I did have some significant experience in journalism. I interned at Congressional Quarterly in Washington, DC, for two summers in 1967 and 1968. My mom gave the fabled Skilsaw back to my old next-door neighbor and family friend Tom Schroth, who was the editor and the reason I got the internship.

For its subscribers, which were mostly organizations like newspapers and libraries, Congressional Quarterly, or CQ, was a periodical that reported on the activities of Congress. It was a serious town with serious professional journalists working for a serious publication. However, I truly enjoyed my job as a lowly intern gofer.

Using my press pass, I would travel to Capitol Hill each day to retrieve materials that the CQ reporters requested, primarily copies of witness statements from congressional hearings. Back then, there wasn't much security, and I could walk around the Capitol and the congressional office buildings with my pass. This was thrilling since those halls occasionally included well-known and influential persons. In 1967, I practically ran into Ted Kennedy while gazing down at the list of documents I was supposed to retrieve. As I backed away and apologized, I ran into the person he was speaking to, who turned out to be Bobby Kennedy.

One afternoon during the same summer, as I was gathering press releases in the Senate Press Gallery, I noticed Art Buchwald making jokes with a few reporters. I was amazed because he was a well-liked celebrity, my mother's favorite author, and the dean of American humor columnists. He would also be my friend in twenty-five years, something I could not have predicted when I was nineteen.

In 1968, a very gloomy year for America, I started my final year at Haverford. The Tet Offensive, a significant defeat in a conflict that the public had grown tired of, marked the beginning of the year. Knowing he would likely lose if he ran again, Lyndon Johnson declared in March that he would not. Following the assassination of Martin Luther King in April and violent riots in several towns, it became apparent that Dr. King's ideal would not be realized for some time. Bobby Kennedy was slain in June. Amid tear gas, Democrats chose poor old Hubert Humphrey for president in August, while the Republicans nominated Richard Nixon. Nixon prevailed in November. He claimed he had a secret plan to bring the war to a conclusion. However, as it happened, not soon.

1969 was Vietnam for me. We weren't out, even though the country wanted to leave and the new president had pledged to do so. This implied that I would be drafted as soon as I finished college.

I was against war like many others. I believed—still believe—that it was a terrible error, an unacceptable loss of both Vietnamese and American lives. I found it absurd that we were still sending people over there to continue the war at a time when the nation had come to believe it was pointless and had elected a president who had vowed to put an end to it.

I therefore didn't want to go. However, I had no justification for a psychological or medical postponement, and I didn't want to act as though I did. I also had no desire to travel to Canada. I thus submitted an application for conscientious objector (CO) status to my draft board.

I probably didn't deserve it. I wasn't a true CO, who is ethically against all forms of violence. I would have left if I had been alive during World War II because I was morally opposed to Vietnam in particular. However, I was granted CO status by my draft board, I believe because I attended a college with a Quaker heritage and because my father was a priest. I was fortunate.

Therefore, I worked in a civilian position that my draft board determined was in the national interest for the two years following my graduation, which is known as alternative service. My final position was as a bookkeeper in the finance division of the Episcopal Church's national headquarters in New York City. Actually. Running an adding machine and entering journal entries for two years was my contribution to the wellbeing of the country.

Even after all these years, I still feel bad about Vietnam because I was spared it while many other men—including people I knew—were not. The folks who led us into that horrible war, lied about how it was going, and took far too long to bring us out are, in my opinion, truly to blame. I still feel bad, though. It was a nasty moment, as I say.

In June 1969, I received my Haverford diploma. Due to the heat, my roommates, Rob Stavis, Ken Stover, and Bob Stern, decided not to wear pants underneath our graduation robes for comfort.

I adore this silly, blurry picture. For me, it symbolizes the conclusion of the first significant stage of my life, the years of my youth and wisdom, when I thought that nothing mattered and that my primary purpose in life was to have fun.

This is not to imply that I ceased being foolish, attempting to entertain myself, or being a wiseass. These were and still are the fundamental elements of who I am. But as I attempted to adapt to the demands of the Real World—making a living, behaving like an adult, and wearing pants—after I graduated from school, I had to temper them.

After graduation, marriage was one of my first adult decisions. For the record, I've had three marriages. Divorce ended my first two marriages. I won't discuss both marriages out of consideration for the privacy of those involved, save to state that both of the ladies I was married to are decent people and that I am solely to blame for the failure of those relationships. Except for the occasion when she forced me to accompany her to see Barry Manilow, Michelle Kaufman and I have been blissfully married since 1996.

Going back to 1969, however, I had no plans for the future other than the two years I would be spending working as a bookkeeper when I finished from college. Despite having a Bachelor of Arts degree in English, I had no notion what I wanted to do with it. I had no actual ambition or job aim. This book's remaining chapters will describe how, in spite of my complete lack of focus, I managed to land the best job any English major has ever had.

CHAPTER 3
MORPHING INTO A HUMOR COLUMNIST

IN THE FALL OF 1971 I was finishing my two years in New York City. During that time I had become a moderately competent bookkeeper and a veteran New Yorker.

I'd mastered the subway system, having spent hundreds of fun hours riding the IRT line between Nereid Avenue in the far north Bronx and Grand Central Terminal during rush hour. I understood the rules of subway etiquette, the main one being that you must never make eye contact with another rider, even when you're mashed together so tightly that you're involuntarily exchanging bodily fluids.

I had learned that, on the sidewalks of Manhattan, even if you're in no hurry, you must always walk with brisk urgency, as though you have reason to believe that somewhere, not too far behind you, is a lunatic with an ax.

I'd become a fan of New York bagels, New York pizza and the New York Mets, who, impossibly, won the 1969 World Series, triggering a wondrous celebration during which I saw at least a hundred people dancing the hora in the intersection of Second Avenue and Forty-Third Street while a blizzard of computer-printout paper swirled down from the surrounding office buildings. On my subway ride home that night, the motorman—I was pretty sure he was not sober—announced the stops in this way: "Next stop Allerton Avenue and THE METS WON THE WORLD SERIES."

So I had figured out New York. But I had not figured out my career plan I had no definite goal other than not remaining a bookkeeper. I had a vague notion that I wanted to do something that involved writing, but I didn't know what kind of writing. I spent a couple of weeks reading the want ads in the New York papers, which listed many openings for bookkeepers but zero for writers. I even went to an employment agency, where a condescending man told me he couldn't do anything for me until I got a haircut.

I was seriously considering this when some friends from my Haverford days, Buzz and Libby Burger, told me that a friend of theirs, Hannah Gardner, had told them that there was an opening for a reporter job at the paper where she worked, the Daily Local News in West Chester, Pennsylvania. So I traveled there and applied. I interviewed with the editor, Bill Dean, and the number-two guy, Bob Shoemaker, stressing my experience as an intern at Congressional Quarterly, which was pretty much all I had to stress. Apparently it was enough, because they hired me, and suddenly I was a newspaperman, raking in a cool $98 a week, before taxes.

About thirty thousand people read the afternoon edition of the Daily Local News. It was published six days a week, Monday through Saturday, and it covered the Philadelphia suburb of Chester County. Twelve reporters, a two-person sports crew, two photographers, and—this being 1971—an editor for the Women's Page were present. In the newsroom, we all sat at gray metal desks, banging out stories on large, heavy typewriters and conversing on cellphones with cumbersome headsets. We kept carbon copies of our work on spikes on our desks, which we never used again. A vending machine that also poured soup and hot chocolate from the same tube served us sour coffee. (I doubt that anyone ever received the soup.)

At the Daily Local News, we were really local. We discussed county commissioner meetings, township board of supervisors meetings, borough council meetings, school board meetings, zoning meetings, sewer authority meetings, police, traffic accidents, fires, courts, and a plethora of other meetings—all of which were incredibly dull. We wrote so many obituaries that I occasionally questioned how anyone in Chester County could still be alive. Events at schools, churches, the American Legion, the VFW, the Rotary Club, the Masons, the Elks, the Eagles, the Girl Scouts, the Boy Scouts, women's clubs, theatrical groups, and the Loyal Order of Moose were all covered in our articles. Locals would frequently ring us with news stories they wanted us to publish. At times, such as when parents took their children to Disney World and felt that the event should be covered in the newspaper, these things fell short of our own expectations. However, these things were frequently considered newsworthy. There was a good chance that one of our photographers, Larry McDevitt or Bill Stoneback, would be sent to the scene to take a picture if, for instance, a Chester County resident called in to report that they had grown an unusually large zucchini and it was a slow day. If it was a particularly slow day, the zucchini might even make the front page. At the Daily Local News, we were local.

I adored it. I adored it right away, and I adored nearly every aspect of it. It taught me a lot, too. During my first few months at the Daily Local News, I learned almost everything I know about journalism. For instance, I discovered that if someone tells you his name is John Smith during an interview, you should ask him how he spells both "John" and "Smith," as it may end up being "Jon Smyth." I discovered that burglary and robbery are not the same thing. I discovered that a grand jury hands upan indictment, not down. I discovered that when you approach homeowners who are standing there, observing a burning house, and ask them basic reporter questions like their names and how they believe the fire may have started, they may respond courteously or they may become angry and yell at you to leave them alone, but you must still approach them because that is your responsibility.

I occasionally had to learn the hard way. You absolutely remember to double-check the spelling of every name, every time, after receiving a call from a distraught widow who informs you that her late husband's name was "Stewart," not "Stuart," as you spelled it in his obituary.

I also gained a lot of knowledge about the interests and disinterests of local newspaper readers. If you write a narrative about a zoning board meeting, you may make a huge mistake and nobody would ever notice. There would be literally dozens of readers, some of whom would be pretty upset, if you were to write a photo caption and mistakenly identify a goose as a duck, as I did. And the phones wouldn't stop ringing if the newspaper ever—God forbid—left out the daily horoscope.

However, I adored everything. Editors shouting, "Who's up for an obit?" reporters periodically yelling, "Fuck!" for a variety of reasons, typewriters clattering, police and fire radios intermittently blaring out staticky transmissions—I enjoyed the chaotic noise of the newsroom as deadline drew near. I enjoyed going to a local bar called Joe's Sportsman's Lounge with some of the other younger reporters at the end of the day, or sometimes even during the day, to drink 25-cent draft beers. We would essentially talk about our jobs the entire time because, to us at least, they were fascinating.

I had no idea what I would be doing when I arrived at work or where I would be sent that day—maybe to a John Kenneth Galbraith speech or perhaps to a fire. In addition to covering shootings, I also covered parades, charity canoe races, the demolition of a smokestack, George McGovern's campaign stop, and the grand opening of a regional sewage treatment facility, where attendees drank champagne from plastic stemware while looking out over the aeration tank. In the early 1970s, streaking was very popular, so I covered a local Nazi group, a large train derailment and chemical spill, an armed hostage situation, and a gas station giveaway campaign where the station was giving away free gas to streakers.

These and a ton of other topics, particularly those pertaining to meetings, were covered. However, it was far more engaging than bookkeeping, even with all the meetings.

It was quite thrilling at times. June 1972 Agnes was a tropical cyclone that began as Hurricane Agnes and pounded Chester County and much of the East Coast. For days, it rained a lot. Rapidly rising rivers and creeks overflowed their banks, causing severe floods everywhere, causing destruction, panic, forced home evacuations, trapped persons, and fatalities.

Over a few days, I essentially didn't sleep. Most of that time was spent searching for flood stories while riding alongside photographer Larry McDevitt. As a teenager, Larry began working at the Daily Local journalism, where his father had been the editor, thus he had grown up in the journalism industry. In Chester County, he was familiar with every politician, police officer, firefighter, creek, bridge, and back road. He drove us from catastrophe to catastrophe while he listened to his police scanner, scowled, smoked a cigar, and tried to figure out where the action was and how to get us there.

At one point, we arrived at Downingtown, where the once-calm Brandywine Creek was no longer running beneath the bridge over Route 30. The town was now bisected by the rushing torrent that was crossing the bridge. Larry began wading out into the water because he wanted to get closer—newspaper photographers always want to get closer—and I foolishly followed him. Suddenly, water was rushing around our waists, and we had to cling to a traffic-sign pole to avoid being swept downstream. We both laughed, but at least one of us was scared.

That evening, the newsroom at the Daily Local News was empty when we returned. I walked to my desk, took out my wet notebook, and began typing as Larry went into the darkroom to begin developing the numerous pictures he had taken. We were both completely soaked. Larry emerged from the darkroom carrying a bottle of scotch a few hours after we finished designing what would essentially be the front page of the following day's paper. We drank a toast to Agnes' survival after filling several cardboard cups with scotch and rinsing them out of the vending machine that poured sour coffee. I hadn't slept well for days, and I've never been a fan of scotch. Even though I was fatigued and wearing wet pants and shoes, I thought, "I love this job," as I sat in the newsroom at 2:30 a.m.

I found my identity as a newspaper guy, which I will always be at my core. I learned journalism from the Daily Local News. I also began writing funny essays on a daily basis there, which is what would ultimately change my life.

On the op-ed page of the publication, there was a feature called Ad Lib where reporters could write articles. Anyone could submit an Ad Lib. Some penned personal writings, some wrote slice-of-life observations, and some wrote on important topics.

I submitted a piece to the paper after only a few weeks there, and the editor, Bill Dean, published it. My first humor column appeared in a legitimate commercial newspaper on November 18, 1971. I've shortened it a little, but this is how it began:

I've been a reporter for the Daily Local News for about one month, so I figure it's about time I wrote a comprehensive article about what it's like to be a reporter. Just in case there's anybody out there in newspaper land who thinks, as I once did, that exciting things go on all the time when you work for a newspaper.

This is not the case.

Since I've been here, not one person has come bursting into the newsroom screaming: "The thirty-foot man-eating iguana has escaped from the zoo and just ate the Civil Defense Office!"

What does happen is the Editor says, "Dave, we got a picture here of the contestants in the Miss Plastic Dishrack Contest. Get on the phone and see if you can find their names. Plastic Dishracks are big in this area, Dave."

Or someone tells me to rewrite the minutes of last week's meeting of the Society for the Renaming of the Grand Canyon, the high point of which appears to be the opening prayer.

And so forth. It wasn't very good. However, it was a beginning.

I was encouraged to continue sending in Ad Libs by Bill Dean, a fine newspaperman and a really lovely guy. And I wrote dozens and dozens of them, each week. Even though I cringe when I read them again after all these years, I can also see the beginnings of my comedic style. For instance, I frequently adopted the persona of Wildly Incorrect Authority—the incredibly self-assured specialist spewing gibberish—a tactic I picked up from the legendary Robert Benchley. I wrote the following in a piece about wilderness survival:

If you or one of your companions gets bit by a snake, don't panic. Take a razor blade and make a cut shaped like an "X," then suck out all the blood. Snakes just hate this, and after you've done it to them one or two times they stop biting people altogether.

This is from a column about how to play chess:

First the two players take their men into the locker room and give them a pep talk.

"Let's get out there and get that king," they say. They never explain why.

I also attempted political satire. This is from a 1972 column about the Democratic presidential primaries, with me writing in the voice of a father explaining the situation to his son:

After the Florida primary, it appeared Hubert Humphrey was the front runner.

"Why, Dad, because he got the most votes?"

No, Humphrey only won 18 percent of the votes in Florida. George Wallace got the most votes, 42 percent.

"Then why isn't George Wallace the front runner?"

Because the other candidates don't like him. They say he's a demagogue.

"What's that, Dad?"

A demagogue is somebody who gets more votes than the front runners. He did this by using a sneaky, underhanded, immoral technique.

"What technique?"

He started saying he was opposed to busing before the front runners thought of it.

"But what is busing, Dad?"

Busing is one method used to achieve racial integration in the schools. It started in the South, and now the courts are saying it has to be used in the North. Most candidates are against it.

"But, Dad, if most of the candidates are against it, how did the idea get started in the first place?"

Well, son, back in the old days, most candidates were for it. That was when civil rights was a good thing to be in favor of.

"Isn't anybody in favor of civil rights anymore?"

Oh, yes, indeed they are. All candidates are solidly in favor of civil rights. But they'd like to keep them down South, where they belong.

I was clearly emulating Art Buchwald's style in that column.

It was fun for me to write Ad Libs, and I was thrilled when people told me they liked reading them. However, I wasn't paid to write columns for the Daily Local News. Even though my work description was growing, my primary role remained as a reporter. After a year, Bill Dean promoted me to city editor, which meant that in addition to reporting, I had to oversee the roughly a dozen stringers—part-timers who received meager compensation to cover meetings in the outlying municipalities of Chester Country.

After about a year, I was promoted to news editor, which meant I was in charge of the full-time reporters, some of whom were much older than me. It was a high-stress task that was similar to solving a jigsaw puzzle on a tight deadline with the phone ringing constantly and sometimes completely unexpected pieces showing up at the last minute. I was assigning stories, evaluating people, hiring and firing people, writing headlines ("East Goshen Board Airs Zoning Change"), and laying out the front page.

I wasn't composing many Ad Libs anymore since I was too busy becoming a news editor. But I was having fun with what I was doing, and I thought I had discovered my calling.

Then, in 1975, I appeared to have made a grave error. Despite how much I loved working for a small-town paper for four years, I felt that I had to go to Big Time Journalism. I thus applied for and was employed by the Associated Press's Philadelphia bureau. I threw a farewell party, gave notice at the Daily Local News, and departed for what I believed to be a better position.

I almost instantly regretted it. I want to emphasize that the AP is a long-standing organization that has produced many excellent journalists and offers a priceless service. It wasn't for me, though.

There was a lot of administrative work to be done because Philadelphia was a hub bureau, a sort of central clearinghouse. This included sorting and routing stories on the various wires, answering requests from member newspapers, ensuring that the sports and weather stories were formatted correctly and distributed at the appropriate time and location, and other tasks. We also recycled a lot of content, reworking stories that had appeared in AP member newspapers for distribution on our wires to other members.

I once reworked a piece from the Philadelphia Bulletin about a sad canoeing accident for the wire. Then someone at the Bulletin, who evidently didn't realize they had previously run the story ran our version. Then someone in our bureau rewrote it and re-wired it, perhaps not realizing we had already run it. I could be wrong and this story—the Canoe Tragedy That Will Not Die—is still out there, stumbling around like a zombie.

I was therefore wasting a lot of time digesting other people's experiences rather than writing my own. When I was permitted to write, I was also required to adhere carefully to AP style, which was generally generic and uninteresting and did not, at least not in the Philadelphia bureau, leave much opportunity for humor. In AP, there was no Ad Lib.

Additionally, I was given a lot of midnight shifts because I was the new guy, which basically involved performing clerical work in a newsroom that was vacant at three in the morning. It was similar to working as a bookkeeper again, but with more loneliness and less pleasant hours.

I detested it. I felt nauseous when I arrived at work and was eager for my time to be over. I wanted to stop, but I was too ashamed to return to the security of the Daily Local News; I had no idea else to go.

For just over a year, I persevered at the AP. My friend Buzz Burger then called me one day to inform me that his dad had had a heart attack and that he needed to hire someone right away. Bob Burger founded and owned Burger Associates, a consulting firm that offered business clients an effective-writing course. Bob and Chuck Meyers, his number-two man, were its two employees. Bob needed someone to take his place as soon as possible because his doctor had ordered him to stop traveling.

I had no idea how to instruct businesses in good writing. However, I hated my job at AP. I quit journalism immediately after giving my notice and accepting the position with Bob. This may seem like a snap decision, which it was, but (a) I was quite unhappy at the AP, and (b) it ended up being the primary reason I became a humor columnist in a complicated way.

I spent the next few weeks in training, which included watching Chuck teach a course at Con Edison in New York and a couple more at DuPont in Wilmington, Delaware, after purchasing a briefcase and two suits.

Then it was my turn to instruct a class. The chemical business Rohm and Haas was my first customer. In downtown Philadelphia, I arrived at the building two hours early. I had plenty of time to get ready by sitting in a men's room stall and attempting to avoid throwing up. I was severely doubting the choices I had made recently. I had a job that I liked a little more than a year ago, but I left it for a job that I loathed. Now, I'm leaving for a position that requires a suit and a briefcase, which I might also detest, and I'm not even sure if I can do it.

I was frightened when I entered a conference room with thirty-two people, most of whom were chemical engineers (a profession I knew nothing about), older than me, and all of them appeared older than me because I appeared to be thirteen years old. However, I had grown a mustache to make myself appear older, which made me appear thirteen with a mustache. For five days, I had to somehow hold these people's interest and persuade them that I had some valuable information to provide.

I made it through. I felt like a phony at times, but I overcame it. I spent the next seven years as a business-writing consultant. Colgate-Palmolive, Sperry UNIVAC, Air Products & Chemicals, Union Carbide, DuPont, Arthur Andersen, SmithKline, and several other companies hired me to deliver the Burger course across the nation. Over time I became more proficient at it. It was nearly always a struggle, but I might have even helped some people write better.

The course's creator, Bob Burger, was a bright, eccentric man with a unique mix of abilities. He was a math wiz and a kid prodigy who could perform complex equations in his mind.

I would tell him, "Bob." Mathematically, what is 397 times 43? After about two seconds of scowling into space, he would utter, "Seventeen thousand seventy-one." He was always correct.

He created a word game called Skink, which he attempted to promote but failed to gain traction, maybe because it required a level of intelligence comparable to Bob's. He was a bad driver but a great table tennis player. He might also be forgetful. He was once upset about two things: (1) his automobile wasn't functioning properly, and (2) he couldn't find his pipe. After hearing Bob gripe about these issues for a few days, his wife, Beth, who is a saintly woman, had an epiphany and found Bob's missing pipe.

The accelerator pedal was beneath it.

While teaching at the Tuck School of Business at Dartmouth, Bob had the idea for a course on business writing. The seminar was based on his book, How to Write So People Can Understand You, which he wrote after deciding to go it alone. In essence, it was a set of guidelines, some of which were outdated conventions: avoid using the passive voice; avoid using large words like "utilize" when a smaller one like "use" will suffice; exclude terms that don't add any meaning ("You need wheat in order to make bread"); etc.

However, Bob had some unconventional rules. He was adamant about avoiding what he referred to as "verb mutilation," which is the transformation of verb concepts into other speech components, typically nouns. Consider this sentence:

We concluded that the relief valve's failure was the cause of the tank explosion.

Although the statement is grammatically correct, the three verb ideas—"conclusion," "explosion," and "failure"—have been twisted into nouns. To make the sentence function, the weaker verb "was" has been pressed into service twice. It reads as follows, with the verbs left intact: We came to the conclusion that the relief valve malfunctioned, causing the tank to explode.

Much better.

I think Bob was correct when he said that verb mutilation was the main contributor to awkward, turgid writing.

I tried to persuade my students that they had distorted their verbs for many hours. However, my greatest obstacle was persuading them to follow another of Bob's guidelines, which I believed to be the most crucial: Always begin with a "lead."

The lead serves as an introduction that quickly and concisely conveys to the reader the main idea of the work. Naturally, this is a basic principle of journalism, but at the time I was teaching, it had not gained traction in the corporate sector.

Almost never did my pupils begin with their most crucial point. They frequently conceal it somewhere in the center, but occasionally they put it last. For instance, they nearly always arranged a report they were producing for higher management regarding a study project in chronological order. An description of the project's motivation would come first, then a thorough explanation of the study methodology, a plethora of data, some conclusions, possibly some recommendations, and occasionally other material. They said that because my project was complex, my managers would have to go through everything from the beginning, just like I did, to comprehend it.

The students would bring in their actual reports or memos for editing in the second portion of the course. I had a lot of discussions like this:

ME (after reading a twenty-page, single-spaced report): If you had to reduce this report to one sentence, what would it be?

STUDENT (after some thought): If we substitute Compound B for Compound A in this manufacturing process, we can make the same product at a significantly lower energy cost.

ME: Where do you say that in your report?

STUDENT: Partly in the conclusions, and partly in the recommendations.

ME: Why don't you start with it?

STUDENT: How would my bosses understand it?

ME: I understand it, and I never took chemistry.

This was a talk I had hundreds of times. I argued that you should explain what you're explaining to your readers before you begin. I n't always convinced my classmates. Perhaps since no one else in the business world seemed to be getting to the point, I discovered that many people in the industry were hesitant to do so. However, I made an effort.

For seven years, I traveled nationwide to teach the Burger course. I improved at it, albeit I didn't always enjoy it. And for three reasons, it worked out well for me:

I first developed my public speaking skills. I had to deal with a tough crowd each time I began a course—a room full of cynical business executives who were expected to be bored. I made fun of the terribly formal language people used in business correspondence ("Enclosed please find the enclosed enclosure") and joked about dangling participles to hold their attention. I eventually grew accustomed to entertaining crowds, which came in very handy when I began conducting book tours, which involve a lot more talking than writing. Secondly, it expanded my outlook. I had a worldview that was centered on the government when I worked in newspapers. I spoke with elected politicians and other government representatives for a long period. Unless their companies were on fire, I seldom ever spoke to them. In contrast to us English majors majoring in journalism who are preserving democracy by reporting the regional sewage authority, I assumed that business was dull and monotonous, and that the employees were primarily dumb drones.

In the belly of the corporate beast, I discovered that while the business world might be dull at times, it is also incredibly diverse and complex, and it is home to a wide range of individuals, including intelligent, humorous, creative, and subversive ones. When I returned to writing columns, I believe this new outlook helped me because I had a greater appreciation for my readers and a better grasp of the society they lived in.

Third, because I had to focus more on the specifics of how writing works, teaching the course helped me write better. I frequently encountered resistance while I was evaluating my students' reports: Individuals with years of corporate experience or extremely specific technical knowledge may be hesitant to take writing help from an English major who appears to be thirteen. I couldn't simply say, "Hey, my way sounds better, and I'm a good writer." I needed to prove to them that I was knowledgeable.

I once got into a disagreement about a sentence's wording with a group of PhD-holding research chemists. In the end, I had to diagram the sentence on the whiteboard to show them that I understood, which pleased them (scientists respect a whiteboard). I doubt I could do that now, but I understood how to do it back then since I had read every grammar and use book I could find in an attempt to establish my authority. And in the end, I believe that improved my funny writing. I started to pay closer attention to minutiae and how even small adjustments to word and phrase structure may change the tone of a sentence, making it seem more arrogant, foolish, or whatever effect I'm aiming for. I can still spend an hour debating whether the word "squirrel" or "armadillo" would be funnier in a particular context.

I felt quite ease instructing the Burger course by the late seventies. The income was good, and the work was somewhat fulfilling. I had reached my thirties and believed that working as a business-writing consultant was what I would do for a living.

However, I had a small side job.

Because I traveled frequently, I found myself with nothing to do and spending a lot of time in hotels and airports. So I resumed writing columns about humor. I typed them up after returning from a trip and took them to my old newspaper, the Daily Local News, where I still had acquaintances, and they were kindly published. I had written them longhand on a yellow legal pad. It was soon a weekly feature, and for the following thirty years, it was basically the piece I would write. As these excerpts show, the subjects were very arbitrary:

What could be more fun than an outdoor barbecue? I can think of several things offhand, such as watching the secretary of state fall into a vat of untreated sewage.

For more than a year now, President Reagan and the Congress have been working very hard on reducing government spending, so it should come as no surprise to anybody that they have managed to increase it.

Let's look at the positives of nuclear war. One big plus is that the Postal Service says it has a plan to deliver the mail after the war, which is considerably more than it is doing now.

The main freshwater fish are bass, bream, guppy, carp, frog, muskellunge, piccolo and crappie. Some people claim there are also trout, but this is a mythical fish, like the Loch Ness Monster. Nobody in recorded history has ever seen a trout, let alone caught one.

I fly a lot, because of the nature of my job. I'm a gnat.

Without question, the greatest invention in human history is beer. Oh, I grant you that the wheel was also a fine invention, but the wheel does not go nearly as well with pizza.

My family had a system for car travel. My father would drive; my mother would periodically offer to drive, knowing that my father would not let her drive unless he went blind in both eyes and lapsed into a coma; and my sister and I would sit in the back seat and read Archie comic books for the first 11 miles, then punch each other and scream for the remaining 970.

This was by no means my primary source of income. I continued to work as a full-time business-writing consultant, earning $22 a column for the Daily Local News. However, I was receiving letters from readers in response to my writings. Some of the letters were critical; these were typically from the Humor-Impaired, a readership I would eventually get to know well ("For your information, Mr. Barry, a piccolo is NOT A FISH"). The letters were generally kind, though.

About a year later, I decided to try to get my column published in other newspapers. A few of my Daily Local News essays were copied and sent to major newspaper syndicates, but no one was interested. Thus, I began mailing them straight to newspapers, primarily small and medium-sized Northeastern publications. A handful of them were interested, but the majority weren't either; occasionally one would print a column and give me $10 or $20.

Then I contacted a small newspaper syndicate in California and they started publishing my column. By the early 1980s, my column gig was starting to feel more real.

The editor of the Philadelphia Inquirer's Sunday magazine, Dave Boldt, saw one of my columns and asked me to send him something. For me, this was significant since the Inquirer was at the time being known as one of the nation's top big-city newspapers, creating a stir and taking home Pulitzer Prizes. Dave published an essay I wrote for him on my junior high shop class experience under the title "How to Make a Board." I wrote a couple of pieces, one about playing bridge and another about hunting, as I remember, since he urged me to submit more.

Then, since it was my big break, I sent him one that I can still clearly recall. It has to do with my son Rob's birth. In fact, I sent it in twice: Dave said, "Make it longer," and returned it the first time. and more humorous. After I rewrote it, Dave approved of it this time and gave me $350, which was by far the most money I had ever received for writing. It focused on the "natural childbirth" movement, which, at least in Baby Boomer America, had essentially taken over the birthing process.

Fathers were not directly involved in the previous system of childbirth, as I explained in the essay: "They remained in waiting rooms reading old copies of Field and Stream." "Many fine people were born under this system," I wrote. However, with natural childbirth, both parents were expected to attend classes in addition to the fathers watching the baby be born. I went on with my essay:

Classes consisted of sitting in a brightly lit room and openly discussing, among other things, the uterus. Now I can remember a time, in high school, when I would have killed for reliable information about the uterus. But having discussed it at length, having seen actual full-color diagrams, I must say, in all honesty, that although I respect it a great deal as an organ, it has lost much of its charm.

When we weren't looking at pictures or discussing the uterus, we practiced breathing... What happens is that when the baby gets ready to leave the uterus, the woman goes through what the medical community laughingly refers to as contractions; if it referred to them as "horrible pains that make you wonder why the hell you ever decided to get pregnant," people might stop having babies and the medical community would have to go into the major-appliance business.

In the old days, under President Eisenhower, doctors avoided the contraction problem by giving lots of drugs to women who were having babies. They'd knock them out during the delivery, and the women would wake up when their kids were entering the fourth grade...

The most important thing to the natural-childbirth people is for the woman to breathe deeply. Really. The theory is that if she breathes deeply, she'll get all relaxed and won't notice that she's in a hospital delivery room wearing a truly perverted garment and having a baby. I'm not sure who came up with this theory. Whoever it was evidently believed that women have very small brains...

One evening, we saw a movie of a woman we didn't even know having a baby. I am serious. Some woman actually let some moviemakers film the whole thing. In color. She was from California. Another time, the instructor announced, in the tone of voice you might use to tell people that they had just won free trips to the Bahamas, that we were going to see color slides of a Caesarean section.

Early slides showed a pregnant woman happily entering hospital. The last slides showed her cheerfully holding a baby. The middle slides showed how they got the baby out of the cheerful woman, but I can't give you a lot of detail here because I had to go out for fifteen or twenty drinks of water. I do remember that at one point our instructor cheerfully observed that there was "surprisingly little blood, really." She evidently felt this was a real selling point.

And so forth. In the summer of 1981, my essay was published in the Inquirer magazine. As many Boomers, my generation, were advancing through the newspaper industry and many of them were having children, this proved to be a perfect time. Almost immediately after my essay was published, editors from various publications—some of them were large city publications—called me. The first contact I received was from a Chicago Tribune editor (whose name escapes me), who wanted to reprint the essay and inquired how much it would cost. I reasoned that since the Inquirer had already paid me $350, any additional money was welcome. "How about fifty dollars?" I asked.

A pause occurred. "We pay five hundred dollars," he added.

I later realized that he might have returned with $1,000 if I had responded with $25, but that was the end of our negotiations.

The essay on childbirth was reprinted in several Sunday magazines, and my monthly column was picked up by a few of them. I was requested to write freelance articles for a few periodicals. Rodale Press, a small Pennsylvania publishing business, approached me about penning a comedy book. I was still searching corporate memos for mangled verbs, still in a suit, and still giving the Burger course. However, doors were opening.

When I received a call from Gene Weingarten, who had just been appointed assistant editor of Tropic, the Sunday magazine published by the Miami Herald, one of them became available. (Gene says that after he introduced himself, I responded, "Can you wait a minute? My child just vomited on my sneakers. Gene informed me he wants to publish more of my writing since he enjoyed my piece about childbirth.

As a result, Tropic began printing my material, and I met Gene, who is—I mean this positively—mad (more on this later). I was flown out by the Herald in 1982 to write about my impressions of Miami and to meet Gene and his supervisor, Kevin Hall.

The city was having a tough time then. There had been significant riots in 1980 after an all-white jury cleared four police officers of beating and killing a Black man following a traffic stop, demonstrating the poor state of racial relations. The enormous influx of refugees from the Mariel boatlift was becoming too much for the city to handle. Cocaine was rampant and crime was rampant.

Miami's reputation as a place to have fun was being severely damaged. Time published a cover article about Miami in November 1981 with the headline, "PARADISE LOST?" "A tidal wave of refugees, a plague of illegal drugs, and an epidemic of violent crime have slammed into South Florida with the destructive power of a hurricane," it started.

I flew to Miami to write about it. After renting a car at the airport, I got lost right away in a place where, from what I could tell, no one spoke English. I eventually located the Herald, a large, unsightly structure with a breathtaking view of Biscayne Bay. I got to know Kevin and Gene, whose editorial advice was to take me out to lunch and then let me explore Miami on my own.

My piece was published as a cover story for Tropic. It started:

It was the kind of assignment that journalists dream about if they lead fairly limited lives: The editors at Tropic wanted me to fly down to Miami and become intimately familiar with every aspect of the city— its culture, its history, its people, its joys, its sorrows—in short, its very soul. They figured I would need three days.

I had never been to Miami, so before I left Philadelphia I did extensive research in the form of talking to several of my friends. None of them had ever been to Miami either. I recalled reading somewhere that one-quarter of the murders in Miami are committed with automatic weapons, which is an indication of a highly technological society, but that was really all I knew.

Now before the Chamber of Commerce gets angry at me for mentioning murder so early in this story, let me stress that in the entire time I was in Miami I never saw anybody murdered in any way. So I want all you potential tourists out there to ignore what you've heard about the murder problem, although you might want to give some thought to the killer toads. But more on them later.

I wrote the story in the format of a standard journalist-explores-a-city piece, except I flagrantly violated the norms of journalism, such as the norm that says you should conduct interviews:

But Miami is more than just weather, businesses and dangerous reptiles. Miami is also people, and the only way to get to know the people of a city is to get out of the safety of the air-conditioned rental car and rub shoulders with them as they lead their everyday lives. I think my findings on the people of Miami are best summarized by this conversation on the street:

ME: Tell me, what are Miamians really like?

MIAMIAN: Well, I would say they are a juxtaposition of many peoples, really—people of many ages, many races, many cultures. True, this juxtaposition creates great tensions at times yet, paradoxically, it is also what gives the city its great vitality.

ME: Hey, that's terrific. What's your name?

MIAMIAN: I don't have one. You just made me up so you could get a good quote without having to get out of your rental car and talk to a bunch of people who carry open umbrellas when it's not raining and might try to shoot you with an automatic weapon.

It was an extremely lighthearted piece that parodied several delicate subjects. Gene informed me that some influential individuals detested it, but it was generally warmly received by the readers. He didn't care; in fact, he found that to be fantastic. As I would discover, one of Gene's core traits is his joyous lack of concern for anything.

By this time, I was writing freelance articles for Dave Boldt at the Inquirer and Gene at the Herald, and both were interested in hiring me as a full-time columnist. According to what I understand, higher management decided that both papers would offer me a job at the same salary of $60,000 and that would be that to prevent a bidding war.

The offer came from the Inquirer's editor, Gene Roberts, who was already a newspaper legend and oversaw what would be called the Inquirer's Golden Age—seventeen Pulitzer Prizes in eighteen years. I went to a fancy restaurant in Philadelphia with Gene and Dave Boldt, where we ate steak and drank a lot of wine without discussing business.

We then proceeded to Gene's place, where we continued to avoid discussing business while sipping scotch and, I promise, watching a John Wayne movie on a VHS tape. Gene led me to the front door when the movie concluded, long after midnight, and while we stood there, me shakily, he made me an offer of employment. The assignment was to write three columns a week focusing on regional subjects.

Weingarten, the other Gene, made the Herald an offer: Come to Tropic and write a weekly column about anything you want. I didn't want to move to Miami, so there was the issue with that offer. Miami struck me as a busy, hectic, and occasionally frightening environment that was not a good place to raise a family during my one and only trip there to write the cover story. After discussing this issue with higher management, Gene informed me that I was not need to relocate to Miami.

Thus, I was forced to decide between the Herald and the Inquirer. I consulted several people and they all agreed I should go to the Inquirer. For them, it was obvious: choose the more prominent publication, the Pulitzer Factory with the renowned editor, the one that reported on my neighborhood. Everyone deemed my decision to accompany the Herald illogical.

The Herald accompanied me. The job itself was one of the reasons. I would write almost every other day at the Inquirer, primarily about local issues. Without a doubt, that was a great job. However, I would only be writing once a week at the Herald, and I could write about anything.

Gene Weingarten was the other reason. It was already very obvious to me that he was (a) intelligent and (b) a crazy guy, and he was going to be my editor. He enjoyed taking chances, pushing the envelope, and spitting the cherished norms of professional journalism in everyone's face. As long as it wasn't dull, he was open to trying anything. He was not afraid to upset anyone, even those he worked for; in fact, he took pleasure in doing so. He reminded me in a manner of my best friend from high school, Lanny Watts: a co-conspirator and fellow wiseass. However, Assistant Principal Sabella was no longer present to inform us that we were not permitted to display our dance poster.

I resigned from the corporate world in the spring of 1983 after giving notice to Bob Burger, who was quite kind. Since practically everything I did after that was too much joy to qualify as work, I actually quit the workforce entirely. I was still residing in the little, picturesque Pennsylvanian town of Glen Mills. However, I was now the Miami Herald's humor correspondent, and I covered anything that piqued my interest.

It proved to be some rather strange subjects, as we shall see.

CHAPTER 4
TROPIC

The US newspaper industry was booming when I started working for THE MIAMI Herald. Newspapers had minimal competition for daily in-depth news and sports coverage because there was no Internet (imagine!). There was also almost no rivalry for classified ads, crossword puzzles, book and movie reviews, comics, and horoscopes. Because of this, everyone, which drew many advertisers and resulted in high revenues, read newspapers. Newspapers were powerful, wealthy, revered, and feared. Additionally, they were trusted, still enjoying the glory of the Watergate crisis, when the public thought of journalists as (imagine!) the good guys.

The Herald was significant. With over 400 reporters, editors, and photographers and a half-million-strong circulation each day during the winter, it was the biggest newspaper in the South. With a breathtaking view of Biscayne Bay, the majority of the editorial crew worked on the fifth level of the large, unsightly structure. It was a typical big-city newsroom: packed and disorderly, with people in meetings, smoking cigarettes, bumming smokes, talking on the phone and occasionally shouting into it, peering at screens, and frantically tapping on keyboards and typewriters. Journalists that practice serious daily journalism.

Then there was the magazine for Sunday. It was situated down a hallway in a little set of offices, physically a few yards away from the newsroom but, in terms of philosophy, miles away.

tropical. What a unique location it was.

The management should come first. In other words, the "management." Kevin Hall, the editor, left shortly after I started working there, and Gene Weingarten took over as head of the department. Tom Shroder was appointed his second-in-command. Because they are both outstanding writers, Tom and Gene make terrific editors: Tom is the author of critically praised books; Gene won two Pulitzer Prizes for feature writing at the Washington Post after leaving the Herald.

Thus, they were undoubtedly skilled with language. Their organizational skills were lacking.

Not Gene in particular. Since a landfill would have less saliva, his desktop was essentially a dump—only more repulsive. Gene chews. The mutilated corpses of Bic pens, dozens of them, were scattered among the vast random pile of items on his desk, including letters, memos, manuscripts, books, plates, cutlery, food wrappers, actual food, and the late Jimmy Hoffa. It appeared that each one had been attacked by a small, vicious pen-hating creature, possibly a shrew, that had a medical condition, possibly rabies, that caused it to produce copious amounts of drool. Occasionally, someone would carelessly pick up one of Gene's pens and—YEEP—hurl it as viciously as they might a vengeful scorpion.

As a result, Gene struggled with paperwork management and, for that matter, other responsibilities that come with being a manager at a large company. Legend has it that a group of officials from Knight Ridder, the company that owned the Herald, once paid Tropic a visit. This visit was scheduled: All department heads received a message alerting them to the executives' planned tour of the newspaper and requesting that they each provide a brief presentation on how their department operates.

Gene hadn't read the memo, of course. The memo was definitely spit-soaked and someplace in the desk dump. Gene was therefore completely unprepared when the suits showed up in the Tropic conference room. One day, he made the spontaneous decision to inform them about the upcoming cover story on a storm researcher. We planned to run this picture sideways to give the impression that the researcher was clinging to a tree, his body horizontal, as if he were going to be swept away by the wind, and we had taken a picture of him hanging by his hands from a tree limb to illustrate this scenario.

Since Gene was having trouble explaining this to the suits, he asked Philip Brooker, Tropic's art director, to show them the picture.

He shouted, "Hey, Philip." "Is the photo of the man getting blown somewhere?"

Alright, so this was a funny, but awkward, situation. It made everyone in the Tropic offices laugh, including the suits. Well, everyone except Gene. Gene was far from laughing. This, in his opinion, was the funniest thing that had ever occurred since humor was invented. He literally burst out laughing as he fell across the conference table, snorting and slobbering. He remained there for a long time, trembling, facedown. Having moved past that, everyone else waited for him to be done.

At last, Gene managed to gather himself sufficiently to continue his presentation. He was struck anew by the life-threatening absurdity of the situation when he stood up and saw the suits still waiting, and he dropped down again. When he eventually came up for air this time, the suits were... gone.

We appreciate your interest in Tropic magazine. We hope your management briefing was enjoyable!

Tropic was therefore not a well-maintained machine. There was a wild-haired madman laughing as he gets ready to flip a giant switch and start an experiment that, if it goes as planned, will benefit humanity in some amazing way. However, there is a chance that it will go horribly wrong and unleash some unspeakable horror, and THERE IS ONLY ONE WAY TO FIND OUT MUAHAHAHAHA! It looked more like the laboratory of a mad scientist in an old black-and-white movie, complete with strange contraptions spewing smoke and sparks. The Tropic mindset was, "What the hell, let's try it." Traditional storytelling didn't appeal to Gene or Tom. Instead of boring readers, they aimed to astonish, inspire, astonish, frighten, and thrill them. Anything but predictable. They were constantly pushing the boundaries and attempting something novel. They were successful at times. Sometimes they were unsuccessful, and sometimes—quite frequently, actually—they annoyed people, especially the management of Herald, with whom they had a lot of conflicts. On sometimes, though, it was worthwhile.

As an illustration: Tropic determined that since both teams were going to be bad for a time, we should start a rivalry between Orlando and Miami's new franchise, the Heat, when Orlando received its own NBA team in 1989, the Magic. I produced a cover piece outlining my careful, impartial, and balanced impressions of Orlando after Gene and Tom sent me there with photographer Bill Wax. It started:

This is far enough. I am referring to the vicious and bitter rivalry that has developed between Orlando and Miami. Too much animosity, retaliation, and juvenile epithets have been expressed. Arguing about who initiated it is pointless. It doesn't help to focus on whether the low-forehead nosepicking yahoos of Orlando or the decent folks of Miami are to blame for the out-of-control situation.

And so forth. The essay, which was a savage attack on Orlando, ended by asking Tropic readers to send anti-Orlando shouts to enter a contest. Gene and I took a bus to Orlando to see the Magic vs. Heat game in the inaugural regular season, and the winners—roughly two dozen people—went with us. It was crazy: The Orlando management, under the direction of the late Pat Williams, the team president and a maniac, encouraged the rivalry by setting up a special sitting area with yellow crime scene tape and baking soda scattered throughout to mimic cocaine.

It was all enjoyable. It was undoubtedly stepping outside the bounds of journalism and into the realm of performance art. However, it was a hit with most people, even those in Orlando.

People were offended by the Tropic cover that accompanied my essay, and some people were genuinely bothered by it. It was a picture of me holding a basketball in a pose. Gene was mostly responsible for the idea. Tom and I both told him that it would never be authorized, but he managed to persuade Janet Chusmir, the executive editor, to allow him to run it. This meant that a half million families, especially those with impressionable children, saw the picture on the front of the Sunday magazine published by the Herald.

Some readers, as you could expect, were upset. A Miami radio-show host launched a multi-day campaign to get Gene and myself fired, get people to cancel their subscriptions, and get sponsors to stop supporting the Herald after the Herald received irate emails and calls. Later, Janet Chusmir admitted to Gene that her worst error as an editor was approving the picture. Naturally, Gene thought it was fantastic.

That was Tropic's management style: intelligent, even clever, but occasionally immature, prone to sarcasm and wiseassery. Tropic generated an impressive amount of high-quality content under this direction. Tom and Gene were a major factor. The authors they collaborated with were another.

The Herald has a history of drawing in young, smart journalists with ambition, and Miami has long been seen as a superb news town. It didn't always retain them; hundreds or even thousands of Herald photographers and reporters moved on to have illustrious careers at the Washington Post and the New York Times. However, the Herald had a lot of skill among its young hotshots and veterans. South Florida also had some excellent independent contractors. Tropic draws from this group of skilled individuals.

Joel Achenbach, John Barry, Madeleine Blais, Philip Brooker, Michael Browning, Edna Buchanan, Michael Carlebach, Pete Collins, Bill Cosford, Brian Dickerson, John Dorschner, Michel du Cille, Tananarive Due, Chuck Fadely, Marc Fisher, Sydney Freedberg, C. W. Griffin, Carol Guzy, James Hall, Vicki Hendricks, Ran Henry, Carl Hiaasen, John Katzenbach, Marjorie Klein, Meg Laughlin, Jeff Leen, Elmore Leonard, Paul Levine, Linda Robertson, Bill Rose, Leon Rosenblatt, T. M. Shine, Maggie Evans Silverstein, Les Standiford, David Von Drehle, Mike Wilson, and others contributed words, images, and artwork for the magazine.

So many talented writers; so many intelligent people. And they have a lot to write. Miami, this wild, exotic location, this beautiful, unpredictable, dangerous, brazen, crazy, turbulent town, was the third thing that made Tropic unique. It was an ideal setting for narrative, and Tropic thrived there for a few amazing years. I couldn't have arrived at a more favorable moment or location.

I played two roles in this endeavor. My primary responsibility was to produce a column every week, which could be on whatever I found funny. Occasionally, it was about my pets, occasionally it was about the news, occasionally it was about a story a reader wrote me about a toilet that exploded, and occasionally it was actually about nothing at all. Like a true reporter, I occasionally actually left my house to write about events, but I wasn't concerned with accuracy, fairness, or taste. Investigative humor was what I was doing. I had an incredible amount of finances and freedom: Gene and Tom would gladly pay for my travel fees to almost anyplace for almost anything that appeared like it may be amusing.

For instance, I discovered in 1984 that the Waldorf-Astoria was hosting the First Annual French Wine Sommelier Contest in America, which was organized by the French wine industry. To spend an evening in a large ballroom with hundreds of Serious Wine People seated at a table with Serious Wine Journalists, I rented a tuxedo and traveled to New York. Numerous courses of exquisite French cuisine and numerous glasses of exquisite French wine were presented to us. This is a passage taken from my column:

We in the audience got to drink just gallons of wine. At least I did. My policy with wine is very similar to my policy with beer, which is I just pretty much drink it and look around for more. The people at my table, on the other hand, leaned more toward the slosh-and-sniff approach, where you don't so much drink the wine as you frown and then make a thoughtful remark about it such as you might make about a job applicant. ("I find it ambitious, but somewhat strident." Or: "It's lucid, yes, but almost Episcopalian in its predictability.") As it happened, I was sitting next to a French person named Mary, and I asked her if people in France carry on this way about wine. "No," she said, "they just drink it. They're more used to it."

There were 12 sommeliers from around the country in the contest; they got there by winning regional competitions, and earlier in the day they had taken a written exam with questions like: "Which of the following appellations belong in the Savoie region? (a) Crepy; (b) Seyssel; (c)

Arbois; (d) Etoile; (e) Ripple." (I'm joking about Ripple, of course. The Savoie region would not use Ripple as an insecticide.)

The first event of the evening competition was a blind tasting, where the sommeliers had to identify a mystery wine. We in the audience got to try it, too. It was a wine that I would describe as yellow, and everyone at my table agreed it was awful. "Much too woody," said one person. "Heavily oxidized," said another. "Bat urine," I offered. The others felt this was a tad harsh. I was the only one who finished my glass.

Next we got a non-mystery wine, red in color, with a French name, and I thought it was swell, gulped it right down, but one of the wine writers at my table got upset because it was a 1979, and the program said we were supposed to get a 1978. If you can imagine. So we got some 1978, and it was swell, too. "They're both credible," said the wine writer, "but there's a great difference in character." I was the only one who laughed, although I think Mary sort of wanted to.

And so on. Writing a funny column was simple. How someone could attend the American French Wine Sommelier Contest without writing a funny column is beyond me. I remember walking unsteadily out of the Waldorf-Astoria at night, my stomach full of good French food and my reporter's notebook full of notes ("BAT URINE") penned in an increasingly unintelligible script, thinking, I can't believe I'm getting paid to do this.

My work included writing a weekly piece on anything I wanted. The second portion required writing cover stories like the Orlando-Miami basketball battle in Miami for a week or two. Although longer and more coherent than my columns, these were nonetheless terribly unserious. Like a tactical assault clown, Gene or Tom liked directing me at a topic and printing what I wrote.

One of my first duties was to interview Florida governor Bob Graham. I flew to Tallahassee with Herald photographer Joe Rimkus for a fifteen-minute appointment. We were in the governor's office anteroom with a dozen others waiting to see him at the designated hour. I felt worried and intimidated. I had no genuine journalistic questions, and I didn't know how the governor, obviously busy, would react to having his gubernatorial time spent by some asshole writer searching for yuks.

His response was excellent. Graham, a Harvard-educated lawyer and successful politician, but also rather goofy. He usually hid it. His solemn, methodical public speaking was boring. I discovered when I entered his office that day that he went into Zany Mode while being interviewed by a humor columnist.

He immediately answered my crazy questions with a slightly gubernatorial-sounding but equally ridiculous answer. The session lasted almost 15 minutes; Graham followed me and Joe out of his office still talking. My cover story was an interview transcript. An excerpt:

BARRY: What can the state do about harmonica safety? I don't know if you have any idea how many Floridians die every year in harmonica accidents…

GRAHAM: Well last year we actually made some substantial improvement. In 1981, there were four people who died of harmonica accidents. Now actually, I think it's only fair to count three of them, because the fourth one was actually, I would say it was more of a swimming-pool accident. He was playing the harmonica in the swimming pool and actually jumped off the shallow end, hit his head, and we don't know whether it was the fact that he swallowed the harmonica, or the brain damage. They counted it as a harmonica accident. Now, this year, or 1982, the last year for which we have statistics, we only had two harmonica accidents. I think it was the result of the public-service ads that I did…

BARRY: The Harmonica Safety Day I think was a wonderful…

GRAHAM: …and we built it around the theme that if you want to play "Dixie," it's fine, but don't do it in front of the air-conditioning duct, because that's where we found that most of the deaths occurred. It was the vacuum that was created.

BARRY: This leads us almost directly to toads. I've been staying at a house in Broward County, and there are, every morning out on the patio, toads the size of mailboxes. What can we do?

GRAHAM: I grew up in the town of Pennsuco, and in Pennsuco, in my backyard we had lots of toads, and particularly this time of year, the toads are really out. And the way we handled them was with BB guns.

BARRY: The great environmentalist.

GRAHAM: Yeah. I used to go out in the afternoon with my friends and BB guns, and that's how we diminished the toad population.

BARRY: If you were to hit these toads in this Broward County home with a BB gun, they would just get enraged, if they even noticed it. They would barge into the house...

GRAHAM: Listen. If you want to just go out there like some amateur, firing away, that's what'll happen to you. But what you've got to do, you've got to wait until the toad raises his head above a forty-five-degree angle, you get that soft... have you heard that phrase, the "soft underbelly"? Winston Churchill was big on soft underbellies, and he tried it in both World War I and World War II. But you got to get them right there [gesturing toward throat].

BARRY: What do you think of the idea of—this is an idea I came up with...

GRAHAM: God, it's time.

BARRY: What we do is drain the Everglades, kill all the bugs, put in nice, clean restrooms, fill it back up and have a theme swamp. What do you think?

GRAHAM: John Kennedy once made the statement that victory has a hundred parents, but defeat is always an orphan. I want to tell you, you got a lot of orphan ideas.

In 1986 Graham won election to the US Senate, defeating incumbent Paula Hawkins. I wrote about that campaign, spending a few days flying around Florida in a small plane with Graham and some national political reporters from big-time papers. In my story I made a lot of fun of Graham's speaking style:

We land in Bartow, which apparently consists of a hangar. Inside the hangar is a smallish agricultural crowd, which Graham, using his oratorical skills, immediately whips into a stupor. He is not a gifted speaker. He is the kind of speaker who, if he were not the governor, people would shoot rubber bands at after a while.

The high point of his Bartow speech comes when he holds up a can of Florida concentrated orange juice, which the crowd applauds, because frankly, and I am not trying to be cruel here, it exudes more charisma than the governor.

"Would you say," I ask, "that spending a lot of time around cows as a child could make a person kind of dull?" Graham grew up on a dairy.

"It could have that potential," he answers, "but on the other hand, some might say—but I am too modest to personally say this—that it brings out a quickness of wit, a sense of ironic humor, an ability to, with a—not a destructive, but a positive uplifting way—with words to bring humor into the world. That's what some people would say. I am too personally modest."

During the Bartow speech, I locate, just outside the hangar, an enormous insect of the type that you would never find in a state such as Ohio. I pick it up, using my notebook, which it spits brown glop on, to test a theory I have about Graham, which is that he will comment on anything. I show it to him, and ask: "Governor, would you comment on this insect?"

"This," he says, picking his words very carefully, as he always does, "is an [here he says a name that sounds like 'Execretius Bolemius,' which he is clearly making up]. It is a Friend to Man. It is a member of the family of Almost-Flying Insects, and one of the many things that it does is that it titillates the toad."

As a humor columnist, I loved Bob Graham. As buddies as a humor columnist and a politician can be, we exchanged letters for years. I occasionally phoned him for Washington's official take on key problems during his Senate career, and he never failed me. In 1993, I learned that a technical institute in Winona, Minnesota, was closing its last accordion-repair program because to poor enrollment. I contacted Bob Graham and…

I had barely got the words "accordion-repair crisis" out of my mouth when he launched into an impassioned oration, from which I got the following quotes, which I swear I am not making up:

"Just last night I ate at an Italian restaurant which, like thousands of other Italian restaurants across America, is now without music, because their accordion is in disrepair and has been returned from Winona, Minn., with postage due."

"We are preparing an anti-dumping order against Liechtenstein, which has become the center of accordion repair on a global basis and has developed some ferociously anti-competitive practices."

Graham was a rising Democratic figure, being on Bill Clinton's and Al Gore's short lists for running mate. He seriously considered running for president in 2004, but health difficulties prevented that. What a shame. A Bob Graham presidency would have benefited America. At least for me.

Graham enjoyed my stories about him, unlike most of my profile subjects. My 1988 profile of Miami Dolphins coach Don Shula comes to mind. He and Jesus Christ were Miami's most revered figures at the time. 32 Gene wanted me to profile him, but he didn't want it to be worshipful. I think Gene wanted me to do the profile because he had a very nonreverential cover photo idea, which I will discuss momentarily.

I sat out with sportswriters to the Dolphins' practice facility every day for a week to witness the huge, sweaty football players. Shula, sensitive about his potbelly and always attempting to reduce weight, would jog alone around the practice field several times after each practice. On a whim, I asked to run with him and interview him. To my surprise, he accepted, probably because (a) jogging is dull and (b) he knew I wasn't a sportswriter and wouldn't ask him boring nickel defensive questions.

I took off my boat shoes and ran next to him barefoot, holding a tape recorder, heaving and puffing and sweating as we ran across the field in South Florida's August heat. Although Shula would have intimidated Godzilla, I liked our chats for two days. I hope he did too. His sense of humor and his willingness to answer questions on issues he would not ordinarily discuss with the press surprised me. An excerpt:

ME: What music do you listen to?

SHULA: I love old ballads. I think Nat King Cole had great songs, Sinatra songs.

ME: What's your favorite rock song?

SHULA: Got me there. [Pause.] That's not the name of a song, is it?

ME: Do you dance?

SHULA: I used to.

ME: Are you a good dancer?

SHULA: I feel I can handle myself on a dance floor all right, but I'm not what you'd call a good dancer, or have natural rhythm. I think that you'd categorize me, if you've ever heard me try to sing, as tone deaf.

ME: Are you familiar with the Elvis stamp controversy?

SHULA: No, and i'm not going to spend a lot of time getting familiar with it.

ME: OK, briefly, the government wants to put out an Elvis stamp, and the issue is, should it be a picture of the young Elvis, or the late Elvis, who was kind of chunky. Which would you pick?

SHULA: [Pause.] I appreciate his talent. [Pause.] I don't appreciate what happened to him in his final days.

ME: So you vote young Elvis?

SHULA: He wouldn't be one of my favorites to talk about. There's a lot of great role models I would rather talk about.

In the profile I talked about Shula's famous, much feared scowl of disapproval—I called it the Stare—and imagined nightmare scenarios wherein it might be aimed at you:

Nightmare Scenario No. 1: You have a hot date. A very hot date. You have Big Plans. You ring her doorbell. The door opens, and standing there, looking at you, is your date's father: Don Shula.

Nightmare Scenario No. 2: You're in the Express Checkout lane, limit 10 items. You have 11 items. Running the cash register is: Don Shula.
Nightmare Scenario No. 3: "A Mr. Shula called. From the IRS."
Nightmare Scenario No. 4: You die. You're at the Pearly Gates. Blocking your path, holding a clipboard, is…

So I teased Shula. I thought the profile was positive and humanizing. Had Shula read it, he might have enjoyed it. But he probably never read it. He probably didn't get past Tropic's cover and headline, which Gene came up with before I wrote a word.

Shula's preseason coaching shot against the Bears was the cover. I flew to the game to stand on the sideline with photographer Brian Smith, who Gene gave highly specific directions regarding the portrait he desired. A true professional, Brian, acquired the photo, which Gene used as the cover.

Don Shula was sensitive about his tummy, so we covered it. Shula disliked this cover. About a year later, I was the MC for a charity event with Shula as a guest. The program required me to bring him to the podium for recognition. I said, "Coach, do you remember me?" as we posed for a picture, smiling. He smiled at the audience and added, "Yeah, I remember you." He did not express this with nostalgia. No more jogging together.

Another early Tropic cover article I wrote about Joe's Stone Crab was unpopular. Joe's, a Miami Beach restaurant without reservations, is known for its succulent stone crabs and high wait times. Except for celebrities like the Pope or Don Shula, you gave your name to Joe's maître d', Roy Garret, an intimidating tuxedoed man who wrote it in an Oxford English Dictionary-sized book. Then you waited in a waiting area with the population of two Canadian provinces for Roy to call your name. On Saturday nights, you may wait two hours or more. Joe's tables were desirable.

When I started at the Herald, smart locals encouraged me to go visit Joe's, one of South Florida's top attractions like the Atlantic Ocean or Don Shula. Almost every local told me there was a technique only sophisticates knew for skipping the big wait and getting a table promptly. Most claimed saying a precise word to Roy when checking in was crucial. Depending on the local, the phrase may have been: "I'll take care of you on the way out," "I'll see you on the way out," "I'll catch you on the way out," or "I'll punch you on the way out."

Most of these sophisticates advised against giving Roy money at the door. That would be disastrous. Instead, you quietly handed Roy five dollars on the way out. Exactly $10. Twenty bucks exactly. It was up to the local expert.

However, other sophisticates believed this approach worked just the second time since Roy would know you.

I decided to undertake some investigative journalism after hearing many smart locals tell me how to snag a table at Joe's. I recruited several folks to go to Joe's on a busy night and try several methods to get a table. The analysis showed that giving Roy money upfront worked best for us. $20 and $50 bills got tables fast and instantly, respectively.

According to my Tropic story, an undercover investigation revealed a method for beating the line at Joe's, which is as complex and secret as ordering french fries at Burger King.

Miami was abuzz with my narrative. That this was happening startled everybody. Buying tables! They thought Joe's was first-come, first-served for years. The editor received letters.

Joe's owners disliked my narrative too. Steve Sawitz, one of them, and I met at a Miami bar shortly after its publication. He was polite, but he said several people had complained. After our chat, he grinned and shook my hand, saying there were no hard feelings.

Slipped me a $1 bill.

I met Roy Garret, a retired maître-d', at a book event years later. He stated my narrative gave him migraines, but he had moved on. We laughed and hugged. No money changed hands.

After two years of commuting from Pennsylvania to Florida to write Tropic articles, I realized I enjoyed Miami. It was hot, chaotic, and unsafe, especially on roads, where everyone drives by their own country's laws—I've joked about this, but it's true. Miami was the most interesting, quirky, and nonboring location I'd been, including New York City. It was a funny fountain.

So by 1986, I considered going to Miami. Other newspapers, like the Los Angeles Times and Washington Post, approached me. The Times flew me to LA for an interview and gave me a position. People were nice, but I couldn't envision myself in California.

It was different at the Post. Mary Hadar, the brilliant and humorous Style editor, interviewed me. Then I had lunch with Post staff, including managing editor Len Downie and executive editor Ben Bradlee. This thrilled me. Many of us newspaper workers from the 1970s saw Bradlee as a Beatle—the cool, intelligent, hard-nosed badass editor who supported Woodward and Bernstein in their Nixon government downfall while I covered the Downingtown regional sewage authority. He was recruiting me for the Washington Post over lunch.

No, I didn't go to the Post. Several reputable people told me I was mad, making that decision difficult. However, I believed writing about politics would be my fate in Washington. I'm sure the Post would have allowed nonpolitical writing, but I'd have lived in a city and media milieu where politics is everything. If I worked at the Post, I would have considered that city when writing columns. I avoided that bubble. Tropic gave me the flexibility to write about anything I loved. My syndicated column appeared in hundreds of newspapers nationwide by then.

I reluctantly declined the Post and moved from Glen Mills, Pennsylvania, to Miami, where I live today, in July 1986. However, Gene and Tom departed Miami long ago to work for the Washington Post.

I published a Tropic cover story about adjusting to South Florida immediately after moving:

Our lawn grows like a venereal disease. The Lawn Man comes around regularly and subdues it, after which there is a period of about two hours when you can walk safely on it, but you had damned well better

make sure you are standing on the driveway when it regains
consciousness and starts lashing out with violent new growth tendrils.
The Lawn Man is named Jorge (pronounced "Jorge") and he speaks
virtually no English, but fortunately I took a few Spanish courses in
high school, and we were therefore able to have the following
conversation:
JORGE (gesturing toward the lawn): Thirty dollars.
ME: Yes.

I had to adjust, but moving to Miami was beneficial for me. Miami
and the state were now target-rich humor environments. As the world
has found, Florida is full with craziness, and I was within driving
distance of much of it.

As an example: I discovered that Kissimmee, near Orlando, was
Tupperware's world headquarters shortly after moving there. Since I
had composed "The Tupperware Song," a blues song I performed at a
Tupperware party in my Daily Local News days, this intrigued me.
Dick Wilson, a Tupperware official, called me to ask me to world
headquarters to play my song to 1,000 distributors after I provided a
cassette to them. My big break!

I took a "band"—Tom, Gene, and Herald editor Lou Heldman—to
Kissimmee for our engagement. Urban Professionals wore suits and
sunglasses. A quote from my column:

I'm the lead guitar player and singer and also (I'm not bragging here;
these are simply facts) the only person in the band who knows when
the song has started or ended. The other members of the band just sort
of stand around looking nervous until I've been going for a while, and
then, after it penetrates their primitive musical consciousnesses that
the song has begun, they become startled and lurch into action.
Likewise it takes them up to thirty seconds to come to a complete stop
after the song is technically over.

The only other normal instrument in the band is a harmonica, played
by Gene. Gene has been attempting to play the harmonica for a
number of years, and has developed a repertoire of several songs, all
of which sound exactly like "Oh Susanna!" "Here's another one!"

he'll say, and then he plays "Oh Susanna!" He plays it very rapidly, totally without pauses, as if he's anxious to get back to journalism, so if you tried to sing along, you'd have to go: "Icomefromalabamawithmybanjoonmyknee" etc., and pretty soon you'd run out of oxygen and keel over onto your face, which Gene wouldn't notice because he'd be too busy trying to finish the song on schedule.

The other two instruments in the band are actually Tupperware products, played rhythmically by Tom and Lou, who also dance. How good are they? Let me put it this way: If you can watch them perform and not wet your pants, then you are legally blind. For one thing, they both are afflicted with severe rhythm impairment, the worst cases I have ever seen, worse even than Republican convention delegates. You ask Lou and Tom to clap along to a song, and not only will they never once hit the beat, but they will also never, no matter how eternally long the song goes on, both clap at the same time.

On top of which you have the fact that they do not have your classic dancer's build, especially Lou, who is, and I say this with all due respect, the same overall shape as a Krispy Kreme jelly doughnut.

We succeeded. Standing ovation from Tupperware distributors. A set of ovenware also received a standing ovation. One of many times throughout the years, I thought, I can't believe this is my work.

1987 was a great year for me. I turned 40, which seemed ancient. I won a Pulitzer Prize for some of my writing, not the Tupperware column.

I never imagined this happening. I enjoy my job, but I never thought I could win a Pulitzer or other media award. I was unaware of my nomination.

Commentary was my win. Gene was at Harvard on a Nieman Fellowship when Tom suggested me and wrote a few essays. His choices were wise. I think my column about my mom's suicide showed the judges I was serious. Another column mocked journalism honors, especially the Pulitzer Prizes, while supposedly covering big news topics. It began:

The burgeoning Iran-contra scandal is truly an issue about which we, as a nation, need to concern ourselves, because

(Secret Note to Readers: Not really! Hell with Iran-contra deal! Let it burgeon! I'm just trying to win a journalism prize, here. Don't tell anybody! I'll explain later. Shhhh.)

when we look at the Iran-contra scandal, and for that matter the mounting national health-care crisis, we can see that these are, in total, two issues, each requiring a number of paragraphs in which we will comment, in hopes that

(... we can win a journalism prize. Ideally a Pulitzer. That's the object, in journalism. At certain times each year, we journalists do almost nothing except apply for the Pulitzers and several dozen other major prizes. During these times you could walk right into most newsrooms and commit a multiple ax-murder naked, and it wouldn't get reported in the paper, because the reporters and editors would all be too busy filling out prize applications. "Hey!" they'd yell at you. "Watch it! You're getting blood on my application!")

And so on. I suggested publications start long, boring tales with "Caution!" Entry for Journalism Prize! Don't Read!" I also promised to split prize money with the judges.

That column probably appealed to Pulitzer judges, who spend hours reading Serious Journalism. They do this over several exhausting days at Columbia University, so they may have related to another work Tom chose. One of my favorite tasks was writing a Tropic cover story about New York City.

Miami had recently been featured on the New York Times Sunday magazine cover. The headline asked, "Can Miami Save Itself?" A City of Drugs and Violence." It depicted Miami as a hellhole with drugs, violence, and racial strife—Anglos hated Cubans, Cubans hated Anglos, Black people loathed Cubans AND Anglos, etc. The story attempted to portray positive voices, but the answer to CAN MIAMI SAVE ITSELF was no.

Miami reacted negatively to the Times piece. Politicians, businesspeople, and tourists panicked. This was partially defensive because the Times piece was partly true. However, many Miamians felt it was old news—yes, Miami had difficulties, but things had improved since the 1980 riots and Mariel boatlift. In 1987 Miami, the Times story seemed outdated and patronizing.

Chuck Fadely, a Herald photographer, suggested to Tom that since the New York Times had gone to Miami to point out our difficulties, the Herald should visit New York City to see if they had any issues as a gesture of goodwill.

Tom thought that was a good idea, so he sent Chuck and me to New York to investigate. We stayed three days. We wrote "Can New York Save Itself?" It was complex, as expected. Some excerpts:

We're riding in a cab from La Guardia Airport to our Manhattan hotel, and I want to interview the driver, because this is how we professional journalists take the Pulse of a City, only I can't, because he doesn't speak English. He is not allowed to, under the rules, which are posted right on the seat:

NEW YORK TAXI RULES

DRIVER SPEAKS NO ENGLISH.

DRIVER JUST GOT HERE TWO DAYS AGO FROM SOMEPLACE LIKE SENEGAL.

DRIVER HATES YOU.

Which is just as well, because if he talked to me, he might lose his concentration, which would be very bad because the taxi has some kind of problem with the steering, probably dead pedestrians lodged in the mechanism, the result being that there is a delay of eight to 10 seconds between the time the driver turns the wheel and the time the taxi actually changes direction, a handicap that the driver is compensating for by going 175 miles per hour, at which velocity we are able to remain airborne almost to the far rim of some of the smaller potholes. These are of course maintained by the crack New York Department of Potholes (currently on strike), whose commissioner was recently indicted on corruption charges by the Federal Grand Jury to Indict Every Commissioner in New York.

We're staying at a "medium priced" hotel, meaning that the rooms are more than spacious enough for a family of four to stand up in if they are slightly built and hold their arms over their heads, yet the rate is just $135 per night, plus of course your state tax, your city tax, your occupancy tax, your head tax, your body tax, your soap tax, your ice bucket tax, your in-room dirty movies tax and your piece of paper that says your toilet is sanitized for your protection tax, which bring the rate to $367.90 per night, or a flat $4,000 if you use the telephone.

And so Chuck and I set off into the streets of Manhattan, where we immediately detect signs of a healthy economy in the form of people squatting on the sidewalk selling realistic jewelry.

Although it was constructed in 1536, the New York subway system boasts an annual maintenance budget of nearly $8, currently stolen, and it does a remarkable job of getting New Yorkers from Point A to an indeterminate location somewhere in the tunnel leading to Point B. It's also very easy for the "out-of-towner" to use, thanks to the logical, easy-to-understand system of naming trains after famous letters and numbers. For directions, all you have to do is peer up through the steaming gloom at the informative signs, which look like this:

A 5 N 7 8 C 6 AA MID-DOWNTOWN 7 3/8
*EXPRESS LOCAL ONLY LL 67**
DDD 4 1 K * AAAA 9 ONLY EXCEPT CERTAIN DAYS*

At 3:14 a.m. I am awakened by a loud crashing sound, caused by workers from the city's crack Department of Making Loud Crashing Sounds During the Night, who are just outside my window, breaking in a new taxicab by dropping it repeatedly from a 75-foot crane.

My story focused on Chuck and my search for the Long Island Garbage Barge. It's forgotten now, but this barge was shown (truly) on Phil Donahue in 1987 as a symbol of local incompetence. New York City ran out of landfill space, so it put 3,168 tons of garbage onto a ship and hauled it to North Carolina to be processed into methane.

North Carolina rejected the rubbish after TV news exposed medical waste. After searching south for a garbage home, Louisiana, Alabama, the Bahamas, and Mexico refused the barge. It reached Belize, which rejected it, then returned to New York City. The media and late-night talk shows covered this journey extensively. The prodigal barge was a star like Harrison Ford by the time it returned.

Chuck needed a good barge photo for the Tropic cover. We took a taxi to the barge, which was anchored off Brooklyn's coast, but Chuck couldn't get a good shot after trying from several locations. The taxi driver, who thought we were crazy, took us to Linden, New Jersey, where we rented a helicopter piloted by Vietnam vet Norman Knodt, who flew us over the barge. The helicopter rental cost $8,000. In the newspaper industry, which is dying, you need three executives' written permission to spend $8. But in 1987, we spent eight grand on a chopper without consulting Tom. Golden Age of Journalism Expense Accounts.

My Tropic story with the barge cover was a hit. It thrilled Miamians. Some New Yorkers laughed at it, but Mayor Ed Koch told a reporter he was unimpressed.

However, the Pulitzer judges may have liked it. I got Distinguished Commentary in 1988, so something happened. I planned to take my seven-year-old son Rob to Key West on the day the rewards were revealed. He was delighted about the trip because I always hired a motorbike down there and rode it for hours with him on the back. That thrilled him.

When we were leaving that morning, Gene called to inform me I had to attend an important meeting at the Herald. Gene made meetings essential, but I hated them. So I told Rob we'd go to the Herald first, then Key West.

Naturally, the "meeting" was a pretext to bring me to the Pulitzer announcements. I won and Michel du Cille won feature photography for the Herald. Nearly everyone in the newsroom was surprised. I waited in the crowd with Rob for the announcement, ignorant. A moment before it came, an editor who hadn't been told the secret shook my hand and said, "Congratulations."

At that moment, I understood I would win a Pulitzer Prize and my trip with Rob would not materialize. I looked down at Rob and said, "Rob, I'm sorry, but we're not going to Key West."

He appeared devastated. I realized I had to help my son as a father then. I said, "I'll buy you a Nintendo." Rob wanted Nintendo games more than world peace.

He said "Really?"

"Yes," I answered.

Then two things happened: Rob, thrilled by the Nintendo news, jumped into my arms and hugged me. Second, Janet Chusmir read the Associated Press bulletin and announced my Pulitzer Prize.

The next day's Miami Herald main page read "Two Staffers Win Pulitzer Prizes." Included were two photographs. One showed colleagues congratulating Michel du Cille. Another was of Rob and me. I'm beaming; he's wrapped his arms around my neck and looks thrilled. Everyone I know who saw the photo said, "It was so great to see how happy Rob was that you won a Pulitzer Prize!" Rob wasn't even remotely delighted about that.

However, the outcome is uncertain. Despite his father's advice, Rob became a journalist. His 2015 Pulitzer Prize-winning Medicare fraud investigations were among his many Wall Street Journal investigative journalism endeavors. Nintendo may have helped.

Honestly, I didn't expect a Pulitzer. I'll always be grateful for the great surprise and recognition. It wasn't life-changing. I had the best job in journalism: I worked for a newspaper that let me do whatever I wanted and had a syndicated column in five hundred newspapers that reached millions of people weekly.

Many readers responded to me. Not everyone liked me. Some loathed me. The large heaps of letters at my Herald office showed I was getting a reaction. Going through all that mail was a big part of my job. It was typically my day's pleasure, not a bother. My readers were great. Even my enemies, I loved them. They all participated in my project. I and my readers collaborated on my column.

So the following chapter is about them.

CHAPTER 5
MY READERS

I never met most of my readers. I guess 14% of my readers were lunatics, so this was definitely a good thing.

However, I loved my readers, even the insecure. We had a long-term relationship via the US Postal Service before the Internet. I received dozens or hundreds of letters weekly. Sometimes I had over a thousand letters in a few days, generally because I wrote on a sensitive topic like Neil Diamond.

I attempted answering all the letters myself, but it was overwhelming. Part-time business secretaries from the Miami Herald assisted me. My mail responses would be dictated and typed for me to sign. This failed. Not the secretaries' fault—they were smart, capable professionals. My responses regularly deviated from business protocol.

For instance, I received numerous lengthy letters, many pages full of words, clearly written with passion but making little sense to me. I would respond with a letter like: Dear [name]: What?

Sincerely,

Dave Barry

Seriously: What?

I often dictated one-word responses. Or I wanted words capitalized, underlined, purposefully misspelled, circled, or (for my purposes) typed upside-down. A sentence might end with??!!!(?) or other nonstandard punctuation. Sometimes I wanted the typist to let me draw a cheerful bird.

The professional secretaries were understandably confused by these deviations from business style, so I spent a lot of time explaining what I wanted ("two question marks, followed by three exclamation marks, then another question mark, but in parentheses, and then leave maybe two inches for a bird"). This negated the purpose of getting aid with my expanding mail pile.

Finally, in 1990, the Herald let me hire an assistant, and I chose Judi Smith. I knew her as a school librarian from her hilarious letters. Judi was educated, funny, and forgave my unprofessionalism. She immediately understood the relationship between me and my readers, and from then on she was my first line of defense against the mail, sorting it into letters I wanted to respond to individually, letters I wanted to see but could answer with a form response, and letters I should incinerate with a blowtorch.

Judi managed my calendar and office phone. She was great at gracefully dismissing invites to do things I didn't want to. Writing a humor column makes readers think (a) they know you and (b) you're a crazy person who's always up for fun. Our columns portray this persona, so it's understandable.

In actual life, humor columnists aren't always weird, any more than magicians pull quarters from ears. In real life, we spend much of our time writing another humor column, which is not as funny as it sounds. The rest of the time we do mundane things like see our relatives or buy tires.

However, many individuals called to reach Wacky Dave. Sometimes they visited Miami and wanted to get out with me for beers or supper, their pleasure. Sometimes their club, organization, or company had a gathering and wanted me to appear, give a 30-minute amusing address, take questions, and be their lunch guest. Sometimes they were holding a party and wanted to invite me to meet them and their friends—a really great group, I'd adore them—so I could amuse them with jokes for 15 or 20 minutes and stay as long as I wanted.

I appreciated that most of these callers were decent folks who wanted to talk to me. My real self is introverted and secluded. I have enough difficulties connecting with my real pals; becoming crazy over strangers, even nice ones, is draining.

This is why Judi answering my business phone was so useful. She could defend herself without insulting others. An expert fender. She was Mama Bear protective, but she treated everyone with good humor and Midwestern niceness (she was born and raised in Ohio), so even when she said no, people liked her and didn't hate me. Sometimes individuals tried to bully their way past her, but it simply ensured I wouldn't do what they wanted. If Judi didn't like them, neither would I.

Even though Judi was a great phone wrangler, her most important job was answering my readers' letters, which I had a "synergistic" relationship with because we spoke about toilets a lot. I was the only nationally syndicated columnist, including George Will, ready to write on bathroom issues consistently. This made my readers happy, and they sent me local newspaper stories. My followers would notify me if a toilet erupted anyplace in the English-speaking world or a snake appeared in a toilet—which happens frequently.

I received newspaper clippings about numerous other strange situations from readers. When writing about bizarre occurrences that actually happened, I often had to tell my readers, "I am not making this up." Because these events were so weird and because I lied a lot as a humor writer. I didn't invent that expression, but I used it so much that it became my trademark, so I get paid $5 when someone else uses it.

I made that up.

Newspaper items mailed to me influenced 50% or more of my pieces. In my writings, I always credited these people as "alert readers," a cherished distinction. Everyone who gave me an article, regardless of whether I wrote about it, received a postcard signed by me stating that [name] is an Alert Reader and should seek quick therapy.

These cards were sent in the thousands. My readers told me about scary stories like Rollerblade Barbie, so it was worth the time.

An astute reader forwarded me the Jackson, Mississippi, Clarion-Ledger editorial "Ask Jack Sunn," which addressed customer concerns, about Rollerblade Barbie. One customer wrote:

Two Mattel Rollerblade Barbie dolls were gifts to my girls last year. On March 8, my 8-year-old daughter played beauty shop with her 4-year-old brother. After spraying him with hair spray, the kids played with Rollerblade Barbie's boot. My daughter accidentally skated across her brother's bottom, igniting his clothes."

The letter concludes those toys lack fire warnings. I must notify potential buyers of their danger."

Jack Sunn replied to this semi-mysterious letter by saying, "Mattel does not manufacture Rollerblade Barbie any more."

Being a nationally syndicated journalist concerned about the issues, I wanted to find out. At the end of one of my columns, I begged for a Rollerblade Barbie, and two of my readers—because that's what I had—sent me these Barbies, which they had stolen from their daughters.

Rollerblade Barbie's yellow Rollerblades with flint wheels, like Zippo lighters, shoot sparks from her booties when you roll her. A spark from the eight-year-old's Barbie ignited the hairspray on the four-year-old's clothes, I assumed.

However, skilled journalists don't assume. In professional journalism, we take a pair of old underpants to our driveway one evening and test whether Rollerblade Barbie can set them on fire with hairspray.

I did that, and I found that if I sprayed my drawers with hairspray—Rave Extra Hold worked best—Rollerblade Barbie's boots actually indeed ignite them. A neighbor came to check on them while they burned. If you think it's easy to explain why you're crouching in your driveway with a Barbie doll and burning underpants, you don't know professional journalism.

I wrote about this experiment in a column. Dan Kellison, one of David Letterman's producers, encouraged me to re-create the experiment on the show to teach viewers the risks of spraying hairspray on underwear and sliding sparking doll boots across it. Naturally, I agreed I love public service.

I flew to New York and attended an Ed Sullivan Theater dress rehearsal a few hours before showtime. About a dozen Letterman crew members and a serious NYFD representative were present. The Letterman program provided numerous pairs of fresh men's underpants, hair spray, a Rollerblade Barbie, and a Rollerblade Ken on a large table.

It was a rough rehearsal. As I later wrote:

The ambience was a lot less casual than it had been in my driveway. Everybody was concerned about the fire danger; everybody was also VERY concerned about how Letterman would react. One guy kept saying things like, "Is this OK with Dave? Is Dave going to be comfortable with this? How close is Dave gonna be? Did we run this by Dave? Maybe we should run this by Dave again."

Many eyes were watching me closely as I spread a pair of men's cotton briefs on a table, then sprayed them with hair spray. Then I picked up a Rollerblade Barbie, put her on the briefs and scooted her forward, sparks flying, and suddenly...

... and suddenly nothing happened.

"Ha ha!" I said, to add levity to the moment. But it was no easy moment. It was a moment only hours before the taping of a hit national show that was supposed to feature flaming underpants. Here we had a set of what is known in the TV business as Stone Cold Briefs.

So I sprayed more hair spray and tried again. Nothing. I tried a different kind of hair spray. Nothing. I tried a different set of briefs. Nothing. I tried a Rollerblade Ken (which we had on hand as a backup). Nothing.

Pretty soon all the observers had changed from being-concerned-about-too-much-fire mode to being-concerned-that-there-would-not-be-any-fire mode. As I furiously swiped Barbie and Ken across various sets of underwear, people crowded around, offering helpful suggestions, including: "Maybe we should preheat the underwear."

At one point, the Fire Department representative, on hand to ensure the public safety, said to me (I swear): "You should use Ken. You're getting more sparks with Ken."

Finally, just as we were about to give up, we got it to work (the secret, discovered by Dan, was to use an ENORMOUS amount of hair spray). As the blue flames flickered on the underwear, Dan and I gave each other triumphant high-fives. I was elated, until suddenly the thought hit me: What if it didn't work on the show?

This worked on the show, thank goodness. Nervous wreck, though. Believe it or not, I sweated enormous armpit stains into my sport coat more than once while pondering if I could set something idiotic on fire on Letterman. Another time, I showed that if you put a Kellogg's strawberry Pop-Tart in a toaster and hold the lever down long enough, it will catch fire and send flames many feet into the air.

An astute reader emailed me an Ohio newspaper article about a house fire caused by a malfunctioning toaster that failed to eject a Pop-Tart. As usual, I replicated this event in my driveway with a sacrificial toaster and wrote a column about it. The Letterman show flew me to New York to repeat the experiment. I succeeded after several stressful minutes in which David Letterman, his live audience, and millions of viewers stared at the toaster without anything happening. My nerves were raw again. An old show-business maxim should be, "You can't promise an audience you're going to ignite a snack pastry with a small appliance and fail to deliver".

A humor columnist may seem like a fun job, but it's actually a high-stress job that requires nerves of steel and the ability to execute under great pressure, like a test pilot, neurosurgeon, or omelet-station cook. This is accurate, but not my point. Without my attentive readers, I would never have known about strawberry Pop-Tarts or Rollerblade Barbie fire risks.

Yes, US Supreme Court justice John Paul Stevens wrote to me on his official Supreme Court stationery! Before discussing his advertisement, let me explain his reference to exploding cows. Due to their methane production, I wrote several editorials in the 1980s warning of cow explosions. I wasn't sure whether any cows had exploded, but professional journalism doesn't risk public safety.

Regis Philbin promoted Beano, an anti-flatulence treatment that "prevents the gas from beans". I tested Beano at a Mexican restaurant, the most extreme field circumstances, and wrote a column claiming it reduced tootage.

A lot of people appreciated that essay, but the Portland Oregonian and St. Louis Post-Dispatch refused to carry it because it was tasteless and disrespectful. This made me regretful and vow to follow community standards.

Of course I'm kidding. It made me want to wrench these newspapers' editors' chains. My chance came several weeks later when I wrote a column about RECAP, an active anticircumcision organization that promoted regrowing the foreskin by attaching weights to the penis.

The Oregonian and Post-Dispatch deemed the Beano editorial too insulting to publish, I noted at the opening. I then explained circumcision:

This is a common medical procedure that involves—and here, in the interest of tastefulness, I am going to use code names—taking hold of a guy's Oregonian and snipping his Post-Dispatch right off.

I replaced "penis" and "foreskin" with paper names for the rest of the column. Was my behavior juvenile? It was. Though immature, it was incredibly enjoyable.

I annoyed several editors over the years. Reader annoyance was my specialty. This led to some humorous hate mail, like the postcard at the opening of this chapter from a fierce opponent of the popular Christmas carol "The Little Drummer Boy." That music is annoying, and not just because it lasts longer than dental school. According to my column:

Oh, sure, "The Little Drummer Boy" is a beautiful song, for maybe the first thirty-five minutes. But eventually it gets on your nerves, those voices shrieking, "Pa-rum-pum-pum-pum!"

For openers, drums do not go "pa-rum-pum-pum-pum." Drums go "rat-a-tat-tat." Also I have issues with the line from "The Little Drummer Boy" that goes: "The ox and lamb kept time."

Really? How? Did they clack their hooves together, castanet-style? Did they dance? Are we supposed to believe that two barnyard animals with legume-level IQs spontaneously started doing the macarena?

I'll tell you this: If I were taking care of a newborn baby, and somebody came around whacking on a drum, that person would find himself at the emergency room having his drumsticks surgically removed from his rum-pum-pum-pum.

Several readers disagreed with me on "The Little Drummer Boy." No music column I wrote aroused the same level of reader animosity as my near-fatal criticism of Neil Diamond.

I published a column about radio tunes that make me want to switch stations. In the song "I Am… I Said," Neil sings with much emotion and intensity:

"I am," I said

To no one there

And no one heard at all

Not even the chair.

Here's what I said in my column:

Is Neil saying he's surprised the chair didn't hear him? Maybe he expected the chair to say, "Whoa, I heard THAT." My guess is that Neil was really desperate to come up with something to rhyme with "there," and he had already rejected "So I ate a pear," "Like Smokey the Bear," and "There were nits in my hair."

Please note that I was not attacking Neil Diamond's entire oeuvre. I think he's a very talented songwriter. I like many of his songs. I was merely pointing out that this one particular lyric is bad.

Well.

This criticism did NOT sit well with the large Neil Diamond fan community, which feels about Neil the way devout Christians feel about Jesus, only more passionately. I got many, many irate letters from these fans, making the following points:

1. You, Mr. Barry, are an idiot.
2. For your information Neil Diamond is a GENIUS.
3. He has written MANY brilliant songs.
4. "Cracklin' Rosie" for example.
5. Also "Sweet Caroline."
6. How many great songs have YOU written, Mr. Barry?

7. NONE, because you have NO TALENT, which is why you are JEALOUS OF NEIL DIAMOND.
8. What about "Song Sung Blue"?
9. WHAT ABOUT "HEARTLIGHT"?
10. YOU STUPID IDIOT.

And so on. My inbox was a fury fest. Naturally, I felt bad.

I'm kidding again. I felt good. You know the expression "When life hands you lemons, make lemonade." Humor columnists say, "When readers send you hate mail, they are writing your next column for you."

So I published a column about Neil Diamond supporters' response to my criticism. His response was more than the first column. Neil Diamond aficionados wrote more, but others agreed with me regarding his chair's hearing qualities. More people wanted to vent their disdain, often in vivid language, for other songs, such Bobby Goldsboro's "Honey," which I predict would lose to Hitler in popularity.

My readers were enthusiastic about this issue, so I hit a chord. In my next column, I announced a Bad Song Survey. It received thousands of cards and notes. I wrote a book about it. I still hear about tunes people detest. Some Neil Diamond fans still despise me. Journalism often requires pointing out difficult truths.

Another time, I enraged North Dakota. While scanning the newspaper, I found an article about North Dakota officials considering changing its name from "North Dakota" to "Dakota" to boost its image. I mocked them in a column:

They don't like the word "North," which connotes a certain northness. In the words of North Dakota's former governor Ed Schafer: "People have such an instant thing about how North Dakota is cold and snowy and flat."

We should heed the words of the former governor, and not just because the letters in "Ed Schafer" can be rearranged to spell "Shed Farce." The truth is that when we think about North Dakota, which is not often, we picture it as having the same year-round climate as Uranus.

In contrast, SOUTH Dakota is universally believed to be a tropical paradise with palm trees swaying on surf-kissed beaches. Millions of tourists, lured by the word "South," flock to South Dakota every winter, often wearing nothing but skimpy bathing suits. Within hours, most of them die and become covered with snow, not to be found until spring, when they cause a major headache for South Dakota's farmers by clogging up the cultivating machines. South Dakota put a giant fence around the whole state to keep these tourists out, and STILL they keep coming. That's how powerful a name can be.

So changing names is a sound idea, an idea based on the scientific principle that underlies the field of marketing, which is: People are stupid.

My column also made fun of a North Dakota city that was trying to improve its image:

Are you familiar with Grand Forks, ND? No? It's just west of East Grand Forks, Minn. According to a letter I received from a Grand Forks resident who asked to remain nameless ("I have to live here," he wrote), these cities decided they needed to improve their image, and the result was—get ready—"the Grand Cities."

The Grand Cities, needless to say, have a website (grandcities.net), where you can read sentences about the Grand Cities written in MarketingSpeak, which is sort of like English, except that it doesn't actually mean anything. Here's an actual quote: "It's the intersection of earth and sky. It's a glimpse of what lies ahead. It's hope, anticipation and curiosity reaching out to you in mysterious ways. Timeless. Endless. Always enriching your soul. Here, where the earth meets the sky, the Grand Cities of Grand Forks, North Dakota and East Grand Forks, Minnesota."

Doesn't that just make you want to cancel that trip to Paris or Rome and head for the Grand Cities? As a resident of Florida ("Where the earth meets the water, and forms mud") I am definitely planning to go to Dakota. I want to know what they're smoking up there.

North Dakotans, proud despite residing in North Dakota, reacted strongly to this essay. They wrote scores of messages defending their state, featuring subtle criticisms of mine. "The people are friendly and warm-hearted," wrote one. "We rarely shoot tourists like other states." The most intriguing message came from Grand Forks mayor Mike Brown, who offered to name a sewage lifting station after me if I visited. This is a rare honor for journalists. No sewage lifting station is named Woodward or Bernstein, to my knowledge.

I flew to Grand Forks in January on a Tuesday night when it was minus 400 degrees. Inside the terminal!

All jokes aside, it was freezing. But the North Dakotans welcomed me and urged me to join in some customary wintertime pastimes, including driving about and parking, which was easy even in downtown Grand Forks due to the many available spaces. Ice fishing is a popular winter hobby, but "sport" should be in quotes. I blogged about it here:

The idea behind ice fishing is that the northern winter, which typically lasts 43 months, eventually starts to make a guy feel cooped up inside his house. So he goes out to the Great Outdoors, drills a hole in a frozen body of water, drops in a line, and then coops himself up inside a tiny structure called a "fish house" with a heater and some fishing buddies and some cigars and some adult beverages and maybe a TV with a satellite dish. It's basically the same thing as drilling a hole in the floor of your recreation room, the difference being that in your recreation room you'd have a better chance of catching a fish.

I started my ice-fishing trip at the Cabela's outdoor-supply store, which is close to the biggest thing in East Grand Forks, and which has huge tanks inside with fish swimming around. There I met a guy named Steve Gander, who had two snowmobiles running outside in the subzero cold. We hopped on and drove them at a high rate of speed, right through the East Grand Forks traffic. (By "the East Grand Forks traffic," I mean, "a car.")

We snowmobiled down to the Red River, which divides East Grand Forks from Grand Forks, and which gets its name from the fact that the water is brown. There we met Cabela's employee Matt Gindorff, who had drilled some holes in the ice. Matt dropped a fishing line into a hole, and within just 15 minutes—talk about beginner's luck!—nothing happened.

Nothing ever happens in ice fishing, because—this is my theory—there are no fish under the ice. Fish are not rocket scientists, but they are smart enough to spend the winter someplace warm, like Arizona. The only fish anywhere near me and Matt were the ones in the tanks at Cabela's; they were probably looking out the window at us, thinking "What a pair of MORONS."

TRUE FACT: Every January, the Grand Cities hold a day-long ice-fishing tournament called "the Frosty Bobber." The first year it was held, the total number of fish caught was zero. The second year, one person actually did catch something. It was a salamander. So Matt and I sat there, "fishing," until our body temperatures had dropped to about 55 degrees.

Fortunately, Steve had brought along a traditional beverage called "schnapps," which can be used, in a pinch, to fuel your snowmobile.

The people of the Grand Cities also honored me with a potluck supper in the Sacred Heart School gymnasium, to which every family brought one of the three fundamental potluck food substances:

1. A hotdish—one word, not two—which is a dish that is hot.
2. A Jell-O "salad," which is Jell-O with some other kind of food—fruits, vegetables, marshmallows, Peking duck—suspended inside it.
3. Bars, which are handheld rectangular dessert modules, usually made with Rice Krispies.

The potluck supper was nice, but the highlight of my visit was the official ceremony in which the sewage lifting station was named after me. It was very cold, but a crowd of maybe seventy-five people turned out. I was driven there in a limousine, and Mayor Brown made a nice speech, in which he compared my work to the production of human excrement. Then they had me tear down a piece of paper taped to the side of the building, revealing a plaque that read, in large letters:

**DAVE BARRY
LIFT STATION**

NO. 16

As I later wrote:

Words cannot convey what it feels like to look at a building with your name on it—a building capable of pumping 450,000 gallons of untreated sewage per day—and hear the unmistakable WHUPWHUPWHUP of North Dakotans enthusiastically applauding with heavy gloves.

I have good recollections of North Dakota, but I don't plan to return until summer, August 17–18. I think North Dakotans no longer dislike me.

Not sure about Indianans. I got in trouble for writing a column about the stupidest state in the US. A business that ranked states by intelligence provided the press release for this column. For clarification, I did not imply Indiana was stupidest. I was upset that Florida was just forty-seventh in IQ. I argued Florida should be last:

The three states stupider than Florida were Mississippi, Louisiana and New Mexico. Granted, these are not gifted states. But stupider than the state that STILL does not really know who it voted for in the 2000 presidential election? Stupider than the state that will issue a driver's license to ANYBODY, including people who steer by leaning out the car window and tapping their canes on the roadway? Don't make me laugh.

I then discussed ridiculous state actions like naming official crustaceans. Indiana came up when I mentioned state nicknames:

Despite nobody knowing what "Hoosier" means, Indiana proudly proclaims itself "the Hoosier State," the stupidest nickname. Possibly a Native American phrase for "Has sex with caribou."

Just two sentences about Indiana. I received many letters from Indiana residents disputing the meaning of their nickname. My favorite came from a man who said, "Indiana has no caribou," disproving my argument.

I received thousands of letters calling me an idiot for saying nobody knows what "Hoosier" meant. These letters then gave me the right explanation of "Hoosier," which everyone has always agreed on–

dozens of various answers. Really. I wrote a piece listing some (there were many):

"Hoosier" means "highlander" or "hill-dweller."

Big things are called "Hoosier".

"Hoosier" originated from Indianans answering cabin door knocks with "Who's there?"

Indiana residents used to shout, "Who is ya?" to boats on the riverbank, hence "Hoosier."

"Hoosier" stems from Indiana families' grand reunions, when moms would inquire, "Who's yours?"

After knife battles in Indiana bars, someone would say, "Whose ear?" and pick up a lump of flesh.

I concluded the column:

When people call themselves "Hoosiers," you'll know what they mean: an inquisitive, one-eared, hill-dwelling Ohio River contractor, enormous for his kind, who has difficult pronunciation but does not have caribou sex. Who could NOT be proud?

That column produced more messages from disgruntled Indianans, but I didn't write about them for fear they'd welcome me to Indiana and place my name on a massive aromatic infrastructure. Men can only handle so many awards.

I received many "gotcha" emails from people who thought they had caught me in a mistake, like the Hoosier letters about the caribou. These emails said, "Perhaps, Mr. Barry, before you write your newspaper column, you should do some research, because the lightbulb was NOT invented by Abraham Lincoln."

No matter how obviously joking I was, people would be outraged and correct me if I wrote a piece with a completely false statement. I published a column about visiting France and mentioned "some of the famous tourist attractions of Paris, such as the Arc de Triomphe, Notre Dame and the Leaning Tower of Pisa." You cannot imagine how many people wrote to me to say that the Leaning Tower of Pisa is in Italy, not Paris. People, lots of people. I signed and submitted a form-letter response to so many folks. This letter corrected them, saying the

Leaning Tower of Pisa was transported to Paris in 1994. Ha ha! THAT would show everyone I was joking, right?

Wrong. A Kansas woman replied to my form letter indignantly: "I still don't believe the real original Leaning Tower of Pisa was or ever will be moved to Paris. First, I think Pisa, Italy, would never accept it. Moving the genuine Tower of Pisa from Pisa, Italy, would be too expensive. I asked a travel agent about Tower's shift. Naturally they hadn't."

Yes, she contacted a travel agency. She got me!

Like her, I liked readers.

This column usually generated gotcha letters when I wrote as Mister Language Person. My fictional character claimed to be the world's foremost grammar, punctuation, and writing guru. Mister Language Person answered my made-up queries for most of the column. A few examples:

A. The apostrophe is used mainly in hand-lettered small-business signs to alert the reader that an "s" is coming up at the end of a word, as in: WE DO NOT EXCEPT PERSONAL CHECK'S, or: NOT RESPONSIBLE FOR ANY ITEM'S. Another important grammar concept to bear in mind when creating hand-lettered small-business signs is that you should put quotation marks around random words for decoration, as in "TRY" OUR HOT DOG'S, or even TRY "OUR" HOT DOG'S.

Q. What is the proper way to begin a formal letter?

A. The proper beginning, or "salutatorian," for a formal business letter is: "Dear Mr. or Ms. Bob Johnson as the Case May Be." This should be followed by a small dab of imported mustard.

Q. What if the person's name is not "Bob Johnson"?

A. Then he or she will just have to change it.

Q. What is the correct way to conclude a formal business letter to a cable television company?

A. "I Spit on Your Billing Department."

Q. I am a top business executive writing an important memo, and I wish to know if the following wording is correct: "As far as sales, you're figures do not jive with our parameters."

A. You have made the common grammatical error of using the fricative infundibular tense following a third-person corpuscular imprecation. The correct wording is: "As far as sales, your fired."

Q. I, am never sure, when, to use, commas.

A. You should use a comma whenever you have a need to pause in a sentence.

EXAMPLE: "So me and Tiffany were at the mall and she ate like four of those big fudge squares which is why her butt is the size of a Volkswagen Jetta I don't know WHAT Jason sees in, wait a minute I'm getting another call."

Q. What is the correct spelling of the word "liaison"?

A. Nobody knows.

Q. I work in Customer Service, and my co-workers and I are having a big debate about whether we should say that your call is "very" important to us, or "extremely" important to us. We argue about this all day! My question is, how do we stop these stupid phones from ringing?

A. Someone will answer your question "momentarily."

Q. As an attorney, I wish to know the correct legal way to say "I don't know."

A. There is no legal way for an attorney to say this.

Q. Thank you.

A. That will be $400.

Q. What does "decimate" mean?

A. This often-misunderstood word is an anterior cruciate predicate that should be used in conjugal phrases, as follows: "Noreen was totally decimated when she found Vern wearing her good pantyhose."

Q. What is the proper format for a formal wedding invitation?

A A formal wedding invitation should come in a squarish envelope, inside which should be several increasingly small envelopes accompanied by some sheets of what appears to be Soviet Union toilet paper. Also there should be various cards on which all the numbers are spelled out, as in "at Four O'clock on the Seventeenth of June, Nineteen Hundred Ninety Six" and "Two Hundred Ninety Eight Harbour Oaks Manour Court Drive Terrace, Next To The Seven-Eleven." This information should be written in a high-class style of penmanship so difficult to read that many guests show up in the wrong state.

Q. What do The Dalai Lama's friends call him in informal social settings?

A. They just call him by his first name.

Q. They call him "The"?

A. Yes. They say, "Hey, The! Don't hog all the Tater Tots!"

Q. As a fourth-year medical student, I wonder if there is a way to remember the difference between "prostrate" and "prostate."

A. We contacted the Mayo Clinic, which informs us that surgeons there use this simple poem: "If two 'R's are found, it is down on the ground / If one 'R' is on hand, then it is a gland."

Q. What about "transpire" vs. "perspire"?

A. That one still has them stumped.

Q. I am a real-estate developer building a residential subdivision on a former landfill, and I can't decide which name would be more prestigious: "The Oaks at Hampton Chase Manor," or "The Estates of the Falls of the Landings of Hunters Run."

A. How recently was the property used as a landfill?

Q. In some of the yards, you can still see fridges sticking out of dirt.

A. We would recommend "The Knolls at Cheshire Pointe Landings on the Greene."

Most Mister Language Person columns ended with Tips for Writers, such as:

TIP: When writing a résumé, be sure to use "power words" to describe your accomplishments and skills:

Wrong: "I supervised a team of 15 data-entry clerks."

Right: "I can snap your spine like a toothpick."

TIP In writing a letter of recommendation for an employee, be sure to give it a "positive spin."

Wrong: Bob occasionally has a problem with his temper.

Right: Bob took full responsibility for the firebomb in Accounts Receivable.

TIP: When choosing a title for a novel, try to come up with something that will really "grab" potential readers.

Weak: The Death Corpse.

Strong: The Death Corpse by Stephen King.

TIP: A good way to "liven up" a novel's plot is to give the characters some romantic interest.

Wrong: Doreen entered the room.

Right: Doreen entered the room and had sex with Roger.

Mister Language Person was notoriously wrong. His error was stunning. Everything he said was wrong. He often made three or four mistakes in a sentence. He almost never said anything right.

This made his gotcha letters from angry readers—who presumably thought he was a language expert—so hilarious. These readers would tear the column they were upset about from their local newspaper and circle, often in red ink, anything Mister Language said that disturbed them. Obviously, one thing.

Yes, exactly: These readers found an error in a column full of errors. And they were furious.

"I don't understand how you can call yourself an expert," they wrote, "because 'decimate' does not mean..."

And so on. Mister Language Person upset many. His constant wrongdoing may not have led to the public's sharp drop in newspaper sector respect. I like to think so.

I appreciated Mr. Language Person's critics' mail, as well as Neil Diamond fans', the lady who asked a travel agency if the Leaning Tower of Pisa had been transported to Paris, and Indiana's caribou-loving inhabitants. I liked most of my hate mail.

But I'm glad these people weren't my main readers since my column wouldn't have survived. God bless them, most of my readers got the jokes and gave me quirky, frequently toilet-related news for columns. When I asked my readers to join me in crusades like the one against telemarketing, they gladly replied.

I started this campaign in 2003 with a column about the National Do Not Call Registry, a federal program that blocks telemarketers from calling people who don't want to be reached. In 2003, Americans were sick of being interrupted at dinnertime by telemarketers trying to switch long-distance providers. They would have preferred a federal program that wrapped telemarketers in pig intestines and dropped them from helicopters into shark-ridden waters. However, the Do Not Call Registry was a good idea and popular.

Telemarketers, who were suing the register, didn't like it. They claimed a constitutional right to call anyone, including those who said no. I wrote in my column:

Leading the charge for the telemarketing industry is the American Teleservices Association (suggested motto: "Some Day, We Will Get a Dictionary and Look Up 'Services' "). This group argues that, if its members are prohibited from calling people who do not want to be called, then two million telemarketers will lose their jobs. Of course, you could use pretty much the same reasoning to argue that laws against mugging cause unemployment among muggers. But that would be unfair. Muggers rarely intrude into your home.

So what's the answer? Is there a constitutional way that we telephone customers can have our peace, without inconveniencing the people whose livelihoods depend on keeping their legal right to inconvenience us? Maybe we could pay the telemarketing industry not to call us, kind of like paying "protection money" to organized crime. Or maybe we could actually hire organized crime to explain our position to telemarketing industry executives, who would then be given a fair opportunity to respond, while the cement was hardening.

I'm just thinking aloud here. I'm sure you have a better idea for how we can resolve our differences with the telemarketing industry. If you do, call me. No, wait, I have a better idea: Call the folks at the American Teleservices Association, toll-free, at 877-779-3974, and tell them what you think. I'm sure they'd love to hear your constitutionally protected views! Be sure to wipe your mouthpiece afterward.

I motivated my readers. Would they answer?

Oh boy.

The Associated Press reported:

Sept. 12—Miami Instead of receiving calls, telemarketers review them.

The American Teleservices Association isn't laughing at Dave Barry after the Pulitzer Prize–winning Miami Herald humor columnist released the group's phone number in his Aug. 31 column, sparking a torrent of calls to its headquarters.

Barry advised readers to contact and "tell them what you think."

They'd love to hear your constitutionally protected opinions! Wipe your mouthpiece afterward, Barry advised.

Thousands of Barry readers obeyed, prompting the association to cease answering calls. Callers hear a recorded saying "overwhelming positive response to recent media events, we are unable to take your call at this time."

"It's difficult not to see some malice in Mr. Barry's intent," said ATA executive director Tim Searcy, who said the increased calls will cost his group due to toll rates and staffing concerns.

Barry hardly apologized.

"I feel just terrible, especially if they were eating or anything," he added.

My telemarketing piece was so popular that the New York Times reported about it:

Nationally renowned Miami Herald comic Dave Barry noticed American Teleservices. Mr. Barry released the trade group's phone number in his August column, arguing that customers had the right to call telemarketers.

The American Teleservices Association unplugged its voice mail system after over 1,000 reader calls overwhelmed it.

The group's executive director, Tim Searcy, complained to trade newspaper DM News about Mr. Barry's interruption.

Reader response astonished Mr. Barry. "This is the most intense response I've ever gotten," he remarked last week in an interview. Even more than low-flow toilets."

My readers' response was incredible. In my follow-up editorial, I reported receiving around seven billion calls, letters, and emails on this topic. About 99 percent came from consumers who love phoning telemarketers. These customers requested me to expose additional telemarketing numbers, including residential ones. One emailer suggested: "I think we should call them at home and try to sell them the idea of not calling people at home."

Telemarketers said I was nasty vermin filth and a news media member in the remaining 1% of the response. They argue that (a) telemarketers are hardworking and (b) if they can't call people who don't want to be called, US jobs and the economy could suffer.

In the Los Angeles Times, ATA member Tim Searcy said the Do Not Call Registry would be "like an asteroid hitting the Earth." Yes. An asteroid!

Telemarketers may still detest me. I hope they do.

Another column I wrote in response to a letter from Oregon men John Baur and Mark Summers with a dream received a surprisingly strong response. Why not talk like a pirate on a certain day each year? They thought the world would be better. Since one of their ex-wives' birthdays was September 19, they settled. In their letter, they said they had been talking like pirates every September 19 except when they forgot for a few years, but it hadn't caught on. So they asked me to spread the news.

As a columnist usually looking for something to write about without doing any work, I thought this was great. So I published a piece outlining Baur and Summers's idea and encouraging readers to participate:

For Talk Like a Pirate Day, try using pirate slang in regular speech. Consider a typical business office chat between two coworkers:

BOB: Hi Mary.

MARY: Hi Bob. Have you seen the Fennerman contract?

BOB: I have some ideas.

MARY: I'll check them.

What would this conversation sound like on Talk Like a Pirate Day?

Bob: Avast, beautiful.

MARY: Bob, Avast. Are you delighted to see me or have a yardarm in your doubloons?

BOB: You make me want to haul keel.

Mary: Ahrrr.

As you can see, pirate speech adds romance and danger to daily conversations. Join the movement! September 19: Do not answer the phone with "hello." Return the call with "Ahoy, me hearty!"

If the caller complains that he is not a hearty, tell him he is a scurvy dog (or female) who will walk the plank off the poop deck and sleep with the fishes in Davy Jones's locker. I also considered Talk Like a Pirate on The Godfather Day ("I'm gonna make him an offer that will shiver his timbers").

However, this is a great idea, and you, bucko, should join. Sept. 19: Join us. Swash those buckles—you have them!

My September 2002 column showed that the world—or at least my readers—were ready to buckle. International Talk Like a Pirate Day was an instant smash and has remained popular. Some folks talk like pirates on September 19 every year. They mostly exclaim, quote, "Arrrr," the only piratical phrase most of us can think of quickly.

Despite not coming up with it, International Talk Like a Pirate Day seems to be here to stay, and my column helped popularize it. I think others around the world will continue this useless practice after I'm forgotten—a process that's already underway. Yes, that makes me proud.

Speaking of the poop deck, colonoscopies were another great cause I became connected with. I had my first colonoscopy at 61, ten years late. I might never have had a colonoscopy if my little brother Sam hadn't had one when he turned fifty and was diagnosed with colon cancer. He survived because they caught it early. But the alarm was alarming.

I published a column about my colonoscopy. It could be said that my entire journalism career led up to this editorial. How it began:

OK. You turned 50. You should have a colonoscopy. You haven't. Your reasons:

1. You've been busy.
2. You don't have a history of cancer in your family.
3. You haven't noticed any problems.
4. You don't want a doctor to stick a tube 17,000 feet up your butt.

Let's analyze each reason individually. Wait, no. Because you and I know No. 4 is the sole reason.

I discussed my fear of medical procedures and how Sam's cancer made me schedule a colonoscopy. I then outlined my preparation, which included MoviPrep laxative:

I took MoviPrep at night. Mix two packets of powder in a one-liter plastic container and fill with lukewarm water. Liters are thirty-two gallons in the metric system. Then drink the whole jug. With a tinge of lemon, MoviPrep tastes like goat spit and urinal cleaning and takes roughly an hour.

MoviPrep's instructions, plainly written by a humourist, warn that "a loose watery bowel movement may result." After jumping off your roof, you may hit the ground.

Nuclear laxative MoviPrep. Not to be graphic, but: Have you witnessed a space shuttle launch? Like MoviPrep, except with you as the shuttle. You sometimes wish the toilet had a seat belt.

You spew for hours in the bathroom. Get rid of everything. When you think you're empty, you drink another liter of MoviPrep, at which time your bowels journey into the future and eliminate food you haven't eaten yet.

Colonoscopy experience is nothing, I said. It's better than nothing since they give you a very calming medicine. Afterward, you feel terrific. You say, "Hey, let's do that again!"

To close the column, I advised anyone who had been told to get colonoscopies but hadn't, like me, to get one. As an incentive, I promised to mail them a cheesy certificate declaring they were adults and had a colonoscopy.

That column was popular. It may be my most viral writing. I usually restrict who reprints my columns, but for that one, I let anyone inquire. Patients still receive copies of the column from gastroenterologists and other doctors. Many websites shared it. All around the web.

Judi distributed many certificates. Even though she and I are retired and no longer have an office, I still get certificate requests. Non-friends still tell me about their colonoscopies in public. Many folks have shown me color photos of their colons' interiors on their phones. These people meant this as a good gesture, but as the phrase goes, "when you've seen the interior of one stranger's colon, you've seen one too many."

People have reported that my column led them to get colonoscopies and discover major health concerns that needed quick treatment. The column may have saved some people, they said.

Naturally, this is satisfying. I'm not comfortable taking credit because I wrote the colonoscopy column for the same reason I wrote practically everything else: to be amusing.

Over the years, serious, well-intentioned people have told me that my column improves society because laughter is the best medicine, humor is vital in difficult times, and we all need to laugh at ourselves.

I've always told well-intentioned people: Thanks, but I'd probably do this even if it made the world worse. It's probably my sole skill. This is my DNA. Class clown.

Naturally, a class clown requires students to entertain. Readers are mine. The audience was great. They've laughed at my jokes, told me about urgent news, supported my silly crusades, bought my books, and sent me Rollerblade Barbies. Most importantly, they allowed me to go decades without a job. I appreciate my faithful readers.

I appreciate my criticism, even haters. Despite your dislike of me, you've entertained and informed me. When you've made valid criticisms of me or my work, I've listened, which has helped me.

More than the chair.

CHAPTER 6
POLITICS

The Miami Herald dispatched me to New Hampshire in February 1984 to write presidential primary stories.

Not everyone at Herald liked the concept. As an icebreaker, one of the newspaper editors, an old-school hardass, called me into his office in Miami and asked, "Are you a flake?"

I inquired about his meaning. He meant: Could I, a humorist writing a weekly fun and occasionally nonfactual column for the odd Tropic magazine, be expected to write daily, on-time essays about a significant news topic for the newspaper's front section?

As a former reporter, I assumed I could meet deadlines. He seemed skeptical, and I later realized he was not alone. However, Herald executive editor Heath Meriwether supported me, so I went.

I campaigned in New Hampshire for two weeks. I stayed in an old motel in Manchester's outskirts where you go outside when you open your door. I had a rental car, a map, and the Manchester Union-Leader, which provided a candidate appearance schedule daily, but no primary election coverage instructions. I drove around the little state, attending two or three campaign events a day, looking for funny.

I went to the Bedford Sheraton Wayfarer at night, where most of the national political journalists gathered at the bar. After finishing their stories or columns, print journalists would go to the Wayfarer for a cocktail or three, discuss the political situation with other press corps members, and formulate the conventional wisdom, which would then appear in almost every newspaper in the nation and was often wrong.

Now that everyone has a gnat's attention span, political reporters can't stop reporting, tweeting, and retweeting, thus they can't relax. They spend too much time on screens. Although they drink less and have more access to scientific polling data than the old press corps, they're nevertheless wrong as often. They lack the Sheraton Wayfarer's sociability.

I feel sorry for them because it was wonderful. The Oscars for political junkies. R. W. "Johnny" Apple, David Broder, Dan Balz, Jack Germond, Joe Klein, and Curtis Wilkie were among the big-foot pundits. All the large publications had political reporters, jaded guys who appeared to have been around since Lincoln debated Douglas. Campaign officials and hired-gun consultants worked the crowd. Sometimes a candidate showed up. Network TV personalities like Tom Brokaw may sit at the bar like average people as Election Day approached.

The Wayfarer scenario was nice. New Hampshire candidates and voters played campaign Kabuki on the campaign route, which was the actual entertainment.

A typical event might involve a politician visiting a restaurant, factory, house, shopping mall, or bowling alley where New Hampshire voters had gathered to see the candidate and get free food.

Usually, the candidate arrived late, weary, hoarse, and with a viral illness from too many seventeen-hour days on the campaign trail, but smiling like a crazy on speed. The candidate would be accompanied by several unsmiling staff members, who were even sicker and more tired than the candidate, and a gang of grumpy press members, also unhealthy from living on fast food and following the candidate around New Hampshire, a place they had grown to hate, in crowded vans smelling like Egg McMuffin farts to yet another campaign event where they must lie. The candidate would carry a baby, eat a strange local meal like "poutine," bowl, put on a cap, flip pancakes, or do something else degrading for the cameras to finish the Kabuki.

The saddest candidate events were those without voters. One of my first stories from New Hampshire covered Reubin Askew, a former Florida governor and one of six Democratic candidates. He had a great resume but no chance.

Presidential candidates often have solid qualifications and could do a good job as president, but for various reasons—like Askew's almost life-threatening lack of charisma—fail to fire up the public. Winners, governors, and senators who have always succeeded believe that if voters saw them in person, looked them in the eye, and heard them explain their Vision for the Future, Blueprint for America, six-point, seven-point, or eight-point plan, they would be won over. A groundswell would occur! Why not? Jimmy Carter experienced it!

These accomplished, confident winners come to New Hampshire, only to see their presidential hopes smashed like a bunny rabbit under an anvil. That's what Askew was doing when I noticed him:

I caught up with the Reubin Askew campaign in Concord, where he was touring a shopping center and attracting about as much attention as a demonstration of nonstick cooking pots. It was a sad thing to watch: he has this knot of reporters around him, and they keep asking him, in about 700,000 different ways, if he plans to drop out of the race, and he keeps trying to get through them to find a voter or two to shake hands with. I wanted to go up and hug him.

Askew dropped out after finishing last in New Hampshire. Another candidate who did not do well there was John Glenn, a US senator from Ohio and former astronaut. He'd been expected to be a strong challenger for the Democratic nomination, but he was struggling, as I wrote:

I went to downtown Manchester to watch the John Glenn campaign falter. These days we professional journalists refer to it formally as the Faltering Glenn Campaign, because Glenn is trailing Walter Mondale in the polls.

Don't get me wrong here: I like Glenn fine. It's just that he doesn't electrify the crowd, if you know what I mean. I doubt he could electrify a fish tank if he threw a toaster into it.

Some Herald employees were offended by my primary coverage, notably the Glenn and toaster column. Heath Meriwether, Herald executive editor, called me in New Hampshire. He decided to write about me in his weekly piece. A Herald editorial board member had written to him that my New Hampshire stories should not be published alongside our serious campaign reporting. Heath read me the letter, which stated that treating serious matters like a comedy can damage our reputation as a serious newspaper. I think such treatment reassures the people that political cynicism is smart. I don't think good newspapers do that."

Heath asked me to respond, which was: If you think the New Hampshire primary isn't funny, come see it in person. As for whether it's smart to be cynical about politics, I still believe that our politicians are the most cynical.

I attended the 1984 national conventions and continued writing political editorials for the Herald. The Democrats met in San Francisco, where I reported:

For the benefit of those of you who are just now emerging from comas, the big news here is that Walter Mondale has chosen New York Rep. Geraldine Ferraro, an avowed woman, to be his running mate. This followed a lengthy selection process in which Mondale invited members of every popular minority group to his home, where he would interview them to find out if they were compatible with his views:

MONDALE: So, tell me: Which minority group do you belong to?

INTERVIEWEE: I'm a Black person.

MONDALE: Fine. And how long have you been in this group?

INTERVIEWEE: Forty-seven years.

MONDALE: Very good. Now as you can see, my aides have arranged a complete set of my views over on the dining table. Do you see any view that you would be incompatible with?

INTERVIEWEE: Let's see… that one looks OK, and that one, and…

MONDALE: Could you step it up a bit? Because, very frankly, we have minority groups backed out onto the lawn.

I covered San Francisco street protests. Outside political conventions, protests never appear to accomplish anything other than upset bystanders:

Large crowds with signs demanding action continue to roam the streets. Labor and LGBT have formed the largest clots, marching to emphasize their demands. They demanded:

Ronald Reagan should be dumped in a dumpster and packed with concrete.

Gays: Then drop it from a great height on Rev. Jerry Falwell.

At the Republican convention in Dallas, Ronald Reagan was renominated in a spectacular display of red, white, and blue Mylar confetti on a crowd of patriotic adolescents. The Republicans want to recapture the indoor record for Mindless Patriotism Displays, which was snatched from them last month by the Democrats in San Francisco. Democrats were formerly uncontested in patriotism. At three a.m., amidst marijuana smoke, they nominated their presidential candidates, usually George McGovern, who called on Cuba to invade the US, and Eldridge Cleaver spit on a Bible for the closing ceremony. Democratic Party officials noticed a sudden increase in national pride due to patriotic Olympics-related beer advertising. At their convention, they gave delegates thousands of flags to wave patriotically. Democrats were rusty because they hadn't waved flags in a while ("No no NO!"). They ultimately got the hang of it and established a record for Mindless Patriotism Displays, surpassing anything seen in this country since 1845, when we invaded Mexico merely because it was a foreign country.

GOP convention delegates were especially entertaining:

On the last night of the Republican convention, Ray Charles sang "America the Beautiful." Does this make Ray Charles a Republican? Ray Charles is a Wayne Newton supporter? Because Republican delegates clap to music, I highlight this problem.

Consider "Hit the Road Jack." A Democrat or regular person would clap to this song: "Hit the road (clap) Jack…"

A Republican delegate would applaud on the word "road," as in "Hit the (clap), Jack..."

Try this a few times in your home or apartment to learn how Republican delegates clap. This clapping approach only works with songs from the original cast recording of The Sound of Music, and I doubt all Republican delegates and alternates own more than four Ray Charles records.

It was nasty mail regarding my political columns. I got almost equally as many messages from Republicans and Democrats calling me an idiot liberal communist Democrat and conservative fascist

Republican, respectively. 52 However, many readers liked my coverage, and I enjoyed writing about presidential races. I attended the Iowa caucuses, New Hampshire primary, and both national conventions every four years until COVID-19 in 2020.

Thus, I attended the 1988 Democratic convention in Atlanta. Since Michael Dukakis and Lloyd Bentsen were the ticket, no news was likely. A large press corps was present, thus even minor events were covered extensively.

The protest zone near the convention hall was where I saw this one day. TV teams quickly swarmed a young woman walking a pet rat. I counted five. That night, I saw her on a local TV news show, not at the end with the fluff. Woman with Rat! was a conference highlight.

I tried an experiment since that was ludicrous. I asked Seattle Times columnist Erik Lacitis and Orlando Sentinel columnist Bob Morris for help. We made eyeholes in cardboard boxes. We then went to the protest zone, put the boxes on our heads, and formed a triangle facing out.

So three guys stood around with boxes on their heads. I published a column on what happened next:

It took seven seconds for the first newspaper photographer to take our picture. Within minutes—I am not making any of this up—we were surrounded by TV people, radio people and various other media people wishing to conduct interviews, which generally went like this:

MEDIA PERSON: Who are you?

DEMONSTRATOR: We're an organization called People with Boxes on Their Heads.

MEDIA PERSON: Why do you wear boxes on your heads?

DEMONSTRATOR: Basically because that's the name of our organization. People with Boxes on Their Heads.

ANOTHER DEMONSTRATOR (helpfully): It's an organization of people who have boxes on their heads.

And so on. We gave several dozen interviews and were photographed hundreds of times. I don't know how many interviews got broadcast, but our pictures were in at least two Georgia newspapers and the

Baltimore Sun, and were included with a nice write-up about the rally that went out nationwide on the Associated Press wire.

It took seven seconds for the first newspaper photographer to take our picture. Within minutes—I am not making any of this up—we were surrounded by TV people, radio people and various other media people wishing to conduct interviews, which generally went like this:

MEDIA PERSON: Who are you?

DEMONSTRATOR: We're an organization called People with Boxes on Their Heads.

MEDIA PERSON: Why do you wear boxes on your heads?

DEMONSTRATOR: Basically because that's the name of our organization. People with Boxes on Their Heads.

ANOTHER DEMONSTRATOR (helpfully): It's an organization of people who have boxes on their heads.

And so on. We gave several dozen interviews and were photographed hundreds of times. I don't know how many interviews got broadcast, but our pictures were in at least two Georgia newspapers and the Baltimore Sun, and were included with a nice write-up about the rally that went out nationwide on the Associated Press wire.

The AP convention protest roundup led with The People with Boxes on Their Heads. A widely distributed photo showed the three of us in our triangle surrounded by reporters with cameras and microphones.

Erik and Bob published columns about our experiment, so we were well-publicized the next day. Not everyone laughed. About a dozen newspaper reporters called me in the press center. Some of them, from journals that published the boxhead-protest story, were outraged and asked how we had hoaxed the media. I said we didn't prank anyone. We had boxes on our heads, and we said so. You chose this for national news.

Was I wrong? Did we cross an ethical line? Were we mocking the press, an important democratic institution?

Maybe! But that was amusing.

After Anita Hill accused Clarence Thomas of sexual harassment, the 1991 Senate Judiciary Committee hearing on his Supreme Court nomination produced one of my favorite political pieces from the 1990s. These hearings were so big that the nation shut down to watch them on TV.

It was a serious topic, but the committee's personalities—Joe Biden, who loved to hear himself talk; Ted Kennedy, who was trying to keep a low profile after a few scandals; Orrin Hatch, who was hilariously prissy; Howell Heflin, who spoke very slowly; and Strom Thurmond, who spoke Unintelligible Southern—made it entertaining.

Easy column to write; took about an hour. It's a satire, but it sounds like the hearings:

Chairman Biden: Judge Thomas, these past few days have been very, very hard for us all —especially my good friend and colleague Sen. Kennedy, because it is not easy for a man to sit through three full days of hearings with a paper bag over his head—but before we let you go, there is just one more point I want to make, and it is a very, very important point, and I fully intend to make it if I ever get to the end of this sentence, which as you know and I know, Judge, is highly unlikely to occur during the current fiscal year, so...

Sen. Hatch: I want to say I'm disgusted. These are disgusting things that we have been talking about here, and I personally am disgusted by them. Pubic hair! Big organs! Disgusting. And yet we must talk about them. We must get to the bottom of this, no matter how disgusted we are, and believe me I am. We must talk about these matters, the pubic hair and the big organs, huge organs, because it just makes us sick, to think that these kinds of matters would come up—I refer here to the organs, and the hairs—that we here in the United States Senate would find ourselves delving deeply into these matters, to be frank, totally disgusts me, both aspects of it, the hair aspect AND the organ...

Chairman Biden: Thank you.

Sen. Heflin: Judge Thomas [30-second pause], I certainly appreciate [45-second pause] the fact [20-second pause] that [three-minute-20-second pause] my time is up.

Sen. Thurmond: Soamwhoan ben cudrin' mheah widm tan' bfust drang.

Translator: He says, "Somebody has colored my hair with what appears to be Tang breakfast drink."

Chairman Biden: Thank you. May I just add that the top of my own personal head appears to be an unsuccessful attempt to grow okra. But, Judge, as soon as I make this one final point we're going to let you go, because this has been very, very painful, and believe me I know what pain is, because at one time in my career I was the son of a Welsh coal miner, and let me just say, Judge, that when I do make this point, whatever it is, it will be something that I believe in very, very deeply, because I am the chairman, and I can talk as long as I want, using an infinite number of dependent clauses, and nobody can stop me.

Sen. Hatch: How big an organ? How many pubic hairs? These are issues we need to look deeply into, no matter how much they disgust us! And believe me, nobody is more disgusted than I am! I am revolted that we are thinking about these disgusting things, day and night! Tossing and turning, trying to sleep, writhing and moaning and...

Sen. Kennedy (from under his bag): Are the cameras still here?

Chairman Biden: Judge, we know you're tired, and we're going to let you go in just a moment here, just as soon as I make this one point...

Sen. Thurmond: Deah wheah etn lonsh yep?

Translator: He says, "Did we eat lunch yet?"

That show was impressive. Bill Clinton's presidency was like a Mission: Impossible movie, with Bill playing a pudgy Tom Cruise, relentlessly pursued by powerful forces, trapped time and again in seemingly insurmountable predicaments—He can't possibly get out of this one! His semen is on the dress, but he escapes.

I saw Clinton do this in 1992 NH primary. He was the Democratic frontrunner until he was accused of draft-dodging and philandering. The Sheraton Wayfarer bar was unanimous that he was done. My first primary column was on that:

Manchester, NH — Thus, the professional news media has returned to this bitter-cold, windswept, snow-covered state to answer the question that every four years haunts every American who cares about democracy: Can we charge thermal underwear to our expense accounts?

We also care about the presidential primary next week, which should be fascinating given the press now views all candidates, regardless of party, as losers.

Bill Clinton is our biggest loser, having been named the front-runner several weeks ago despite his constant dithering and lack of policy clarity. However, the press needs a front-runner to declare a faltering candidate, so we hired Bill.

I can only say, thoughtfully,: Shut up if you voters think it's high-handed of us to make this decision before any voter has voted. This is an election campaign. The public has no role. Voters should obtain press credentials like everyone else to participate.

Bill was the front-runner for 15 or 20 minutes, then we declared him in Falter Mode due to all these disgusting unsubstantiated rumors about Bill, Gennifer Flowers, Tammy Wynette, Donna Rice, the Brazilian national gymnastics team, draft evasion, and 17 convenience store robberies.

The press has chosen a new front-runner because Bill's poll ratings are plummeting like a pig from a helicopter. We chose—get ready—Paul E. Tsongas, indicating heavy drinking. Really. This low-key individual may be able to photosynthesise, making Michael Dukakis look like James Brown.

However, he is our frontrunner and likely has several key policy positions. But the most crucial thing for voters to remember when contemplating him as a president is that "Paul E. Tsongas" can spell "Gaseous Plant."

I met Tsongas exiting a campaign event a few days after writing that column. I asked him, "How do you respond to published reports that your name can spell 'gaseous plant'?" After thinking, he added, "I see no scientific evidence that that's the case."

Smart Tsongas. He won New Hampshire. Clinton defied Wayfarer wisdom and did well enough to stay in the campaign, and the rest is history. His political skills were exceptional. He represented 1990s politics like Michael Jordan did basketball.

I had supper with reporters and columnists the night before the 1992 New Hampshire primary. We were around ten people who were sick of New Hampshire and didn't want to see or hear about the primary. We chose an Italian restaurant in Manchester that was far from downtown and campaign headquarters.

We ate late and were the only customers when we finished. As the restaurant closed, Dee Dee Myers, Clinton's press spokesperson, Gwen Ifill, a New York Times reporter, and Bill Clinton entered. Dee Dee and Gwen looked fatigued and rolled their eyes at our table. Can you believe he's alive?

Clinton seemed to be having a blast, as if the most exciting thing after a million soul-sucking days on the campaign trail was driving about Manchester late at night looking for voters. He waved and grinned at our table before shaking hands with the kitchen crew. And then he came over to our group and—I'll never forget this—walked around the table shaking everyone's hand, laughing, joking, and saying something to each of us so clearly that he knew who we were. Which I still think he did. Some of us were well-known national political journalists, so that made sense. However, some of us wrote booger joke columns. I swear he knew us all.

Clinton went, unhappy, escorted by Dee Dee and Gwen, to campaign, leaving our table to marvel at what we had just seen. We had spent the past week trashing this guy's campaign, and he acted like we were all great friends. Even though we knew he didn't like us, he managed—this was his gift—to make us cynical ink-stained wretches feel like he did, at least for a few nanoseconds.

As he departed the restaurant, someone at our table said, "Goddammit, now I want to vote for him!"

Another said, "Vote for him?" I'll quit my work to advocate for him!"

Someone said, "Campaign for him? I want sex with him!"

Of course we joked. In some way.

President George H. W. Patrick Buchanan surprisingly challenged Bush, who was expected to be re-nominated, in the 1992 Republican primary. Bush headed to New Hampshire with the huge security, staff, and media entourage that surrounds American presidents whenever they engage with the outside world. I encountered the crowd at a Bedford mall:

The biggest campaign news is that President Bush has an agenda and wants to be reelected.

Within seconds, his campaign began to falter, so he came up here to appear at a shopping mall to get in touch with ordinary citizens living their ordinary lives except that they cannot move because they are being controlled by enough police and security personnel to subdue North Korea. Many individuals, including shoppers, couldn't enter the mall due to security.

"But I'm not here for Bush," a mother with two young children told a mall entrance officer. "Just getting to a store."

But he refused her entry. Ordinary residents cannot enter a mall while the president is there meeting with them due to security concerns.

"I'm voting for somebody else," she stomped toward the parking lot.

On another day, I saw Barbara Bush, who was campaigning for her husband:

In these tough circumstances, hair care is the top concern for American voters before the New Hampshire primary. Barbara Bush visited the Continental Academie of Hair Design, which teaches hair professionals, over the weekend.

Earl Titus, one of the teachers, informed me that the trainees had 1,500 hours of hair-related training, including ethics, before Mrs. Bush arrived. In response to my hair ethic question, he answered, "You don't lie to your client or steal from your client." So it's like law school, except with more conditioning.

Mrs. Bush arrived on time with a merry retinue of Secret Service members who spontaneously colored their hair purple and had nicknames like "Mojo" etched into their scalps.

Of course I'm joking. As usual, the agents stared at you with an attitude that indicated they believed you kept human body parts in your refrigerator. Mrs. Bush, on the other hand, smiled at all the hair stylists and women having haircuts and said she was glad to see everyone. She excels at making others delighted to see them. Nothing worries her. She might be greeting people in a busy room when she sees an eight-foot rutabaga with a BUSH button and smiles.

Barbara Bush appeared friendly, but she was tough and had an edge. When making another campaign trip, she would smile at whatever person, place, object, or hairdo she was supposed to like, but her eyes would say, "Well, this is ridiculous, but here we are."

I know because I was looked at by Mrs. Bush. I attended a donor's home reception as part of the press horde that had followed her limousine around New Hampshire. Her photographer wanted a portrait of us journalists, so he grouped us around Mrs. Bush. I ended up next to her, half-facing each other.

Maybe you've experienced this. You're near a celebrity. This person doesn't know you. No need to say anything—you have nothing to say. The intelligent part of your brain knows this. In one of your primitive brain sectors, a group of cells that perform noncerebral physiological tasks like burping have an idea.

Wow, they think. We're next to a celebrity! We must speak up!

Your mouth, one of your body's least intelligent organs, immediately blurts out what the burp cells consider to be a meaningful thought before one of the better lobes can stop them.

That happened to me at the New Hampshire donor's residence. I randomly told Barbara Bush, in an artificially cheery voice, "I shop in the same supermarket as your son Jeb."

It was true. I saw Jeb Bush in the Publix deli several times. It was obvious Mrs. Bush would not find this fascinating. This fact was uninteresting to everyone. Not really fascinating. However, I informed the US First Lady.

She had to answer as we were just a foot apart. She glanced toward me, and her eyes showed her thoughts: Why would you tell me that?

But she told me, "We saw Jeb recently. Just turned 39." She returned to the photographer.

Mrs. Bush responded graciously. Instead of pointing out my ridiculously inane statement, she pretended we were talking. Naturally, we weren't. Our two statements were unconnected save that they both mentioned "Jeb." However, Mrs. Bush, an expert at handling these situations, calmly got us past my humiliating moment. She saved me.

The smart part of my brain appreciated this immediately. Thanks, Barbara Bush, it thought.

Too bad my burp cells misjudged the scenario.

They thought, Wow. We're really getting along with Barbara Bush. We must tell her something else!

Following up on the exciting fact that I shopped at the same store as Jeb, I told Mrs. Bush, "He's very tall."

This was true. Tall Jeb Bush remains so. For years. We can assume Mrs. Bush knew that. She glanced toward me again, and her eyes said, "What's wrong?" Of course she was too sophisticated to say that. She said, "He didn't just grow this year."

She turned back to the camera, the photographer took the picture, and my interaction with the First Lady ended, which was good since who knows what my burp cells would have done next.

I spoke at Mrs. Bush's adult-literacy foundation fundraiser years later as one of the authors. Michelle and I attended a luncheon for authors at the Bushes' Houston home. George Bush received us at the front door and escorted us into the living room, where he told us a complicated rug narrative. Barbara entered while he spoke.

"George," she told the former US president, "they don't care about the rug."

"Right," he answered, ending the rug talk.

Mrs. Bush was humorous when she wasn't compelled to grin at everything. I eventually felt safe telling her about my embarrassing attempt to talk to her in New Hampshire years before. Although she didn't recall the episode, she told me that I wasn't the only one who had become a blithering idiot in her presence. So I felt better.

Hillary Clinton ran against Barbara Bush for First Lady in 1992. She was brilliant and ambitious, and she wanted to be a policy-focused First Lady instead of a ribbon-cutting one. The polls suggested that the public was uneasy with a forceful First Lady, so the Democrats hosted their convention in New York City that summer to soften Hillary's image. She hosted a congressional spouses tea, which I attended:

I finally caught up with the New Hillary Clinton. She has replaced the Old Hillary Clinton, who was unpopular with the public because she was going around discussing the issues and acting forceful and just generally appearing to have opinions.

This is, of course, unacceptable to the American public, which prefers its political wives to have a stay-in-the-background, stand-by-your-man, worshipful-gaze type of personality, as epitomized by Pat Nixon and most Labrador retrievers.

So a few months ago, when the Clinton campaign was faltering, party officials had Hillary abducted and taken to the top-secret Housewife Indoctrination Clinic, operated by Betty Crocker, where Hillary was subjected to thousands of hours of Ozzie and Harriet reruns and was given massive intravenous doses of Lemon Pledge.

When she emerged she looked like the Old Hillary, but she was no longer shooting her mouth off about matters that frankly do not concern persons of the gal gender, such as the US government.

When I caught up with the New Hillary, she was talking about cookies. This took place in the Waldorf-Astoria Hotel, where Hillary was host to a tea for the wives of Democratic congresspersons.

She told the congressional wives that Family Circle magazine has gotten her into a contest against Barbara Bush to see who has the best chocolate-chip-cookie recipe. I'm not developing this campaign. Hillary told the wives to please vote for her cookie recipe, and they all applauded some more.

Then Hillary started talking about the Clinton-Gore ticket, and her voice started becoming forceful. It appeared as though she was just about to bring up some actual issues when her Democratic Party handlers, standing just out of sight, hit her with a tranquilizing dart, and the moment of danger was past.

Hillary and Bill defeated Barbara and George in the election after winning the cookie recipe contest.

The Clinton administration started poorly. Hillary led the task force on healthcare reform, their main priority. Their idea immediately got bogged down in the partisan muck that precludes Congress from acting. As a libertarian, I support this system.

Washington was fascinated with healthcare in 1994, while the nation was focused on the O. J. Simpson trial. The Herald sent me there to see if I could understand it, which I couldn't. How my story began:

For over a year, the Clinton administration, Congress, and scores of special-interest groups have passionately discussed health care, causing Xerox machines to catch fire.

Despite intense debate, a national agreement has emerged on two key points:

Best health care in the world is in the US.

This requires action.

As I noted, the White House press corps was at war with the Clinton administration during my two days there:

Although this hatred has always existed, it is now more acute. The Clinton administration believes the press has been unfair, focusing on negative stories like Paula Jones' allegation that Bill Clinton sexually harassed her while ignoring positive stories like the dozens of women who have not yet accused Clinton of sexual harassment. The press hates the Clinton administration because it's whining and only talks about health care, which it's tired of since the 1992 New Hampshire primary.

Seeing Dee Dee Myers, whom I last saw in the New Hampshire Italian restaurant, giving the daily press briefing was fascinating. In the briefing, Myers, the White House press secretary, was responsible for ensuring that no newsworthy information was revealed to the press. The press constantly asks Myers questions she has already refused to answer until the smoke detectors go off due to antagonism. The White House press secretary and press corps have a decades-old ritualistic disagreement. It like an elderly married couple still bickering over a 1953 cocktail party remark.

Health care dominated the press briefing. Press wanted to know what "universal coverage" implies. Myers claimed it covers all Americans. This did not satisfy the press, who sought to know what "every American" means. Clearly this discussion had happened previously, as Myers became irritable and declared, "I am not going to be drawn into a debate about numbers." The press attempted to engage her in a debate about hypothetical scenarios, including a health-care bill covering 96% of Americans, a triggering mechanism for total coverage by 2002, and Train A leaving Cody, Wyo. at 47 mph.

Myers resisted. I liked her. Despite her tough-gal attitude, she seemed like a nice person you could go to a pub with and have a few beers with, maybe even discuss numbers late at night.

The reporters stopped defining "every American" and questioned about the dollar. However, Myers would not be fooled.

All dollar comments will come from the Treasury Department, she said. This angered reporters. One of them angrily informed me the Treasury Department was also silent on the dollar. I pretended contempt, but the humiliating fact was that I had no idea what was going on with the dollar. It was not mentioned in the Simpson hearings.

Next came additional testy queries concerning the meaning of "every American," followed by reporters' questions about President Clinton's Camp David travels. The exchange, as best I can recreate it from my quickly jotted notes:

Voice: Why is he there? Can you explain?

Another voice: He fishes?

Another voice: Has he fished?

He hasn't fished, to my knowledge.

Is he a smoker?

MYERS: He chews one.

But he doesn't inhale!

[Laughter]

Many innovative minds in a little room.

After two days at the White House where I learned little about healthcare reform, I traveled to the Capitol to learn what Congress was doing. This was impossible:

Two important Capitol rooms hosted the Democratic and Republican senators' weekly caucuses on this day.

Several hundred frantic reporters gathered in the corridor outside the caucus rooms. They were covering a subject that would be incredibly complex even with one health-care plan and honest reporting from all the major participants. There were several schemes, with fresh ones being established at the present, and different players were covertly making negotiations in different rooms across town about different portions of these plots. None of the reporters knew what was going on, but they had to produce authoritative reports for the next day's papers. Their desperate state.

As senators emerged from the caucuses, reporters formed dense clots around them, pressing close to get the newest health-care developments. I believe Louisiana senator John Breaux was the first senator I saw. He rejected his own health-care package. Multiple reporters told me Breaux and other Democrats were waiting for Sen. Patrick Moynihan, head of the influential Senate Finance Committee, to propose a new strategy. They said Moynihan introduced this plan to get his committee to reject it.

I questioned "Why?"

"Because he wants to show that it can't pass," the reporters said, as if it explained everything.

Sen. Bob Dole (R-Raptor) emerged from the caucus room with a new health-care plan while I was attempting to understand this.

"Tell us about your plan," a reporter asked.

"It's very nice," Dole added.

Do you think I'm joking?

More senators were questioned by media about health care. I was carried up in the enthusiasm, pushing toward the heart of the clump and writing nonsensical messages like "EMPLOYER MANDATE TRIGGER." The media went crazy. If Lee Harvey Oswald appeared, we would have discussed healthcare.

Majority leader George Mitchell was one among the last senators to enter, and the mob jumped on him for comments criticizing Moynihan's plan, which everyone was eager to vote down.

"I haven't seen the details, but I commend the chairman for his leadership," Mitchell replied, showing his capacity to say nothing at all.

Someone asked Mitchell about the Red Sox as he left.

He said, "As of seven days ago, they're five and two."

I typed that down—the only reliable information I obtained that day.

In the 1994 midterm elections, Republicans led by Newt "Newt" Gingrich won Congress and the Clinton healthcare proposal failed.

Bob Dole, a combat hero and skilled legislator who was affable and humorous in small groups, was the 1996 Republican nominee. He came across as old and irritable when giving presentations, like a person moaning that someone took his egg-salad sandwich from the office refrigerator. Clinton handily won the 1996 election, defeating him.

Clinton's second term was dominated by the Republican Congress' passionate but incompetent attempt to impeach him on constitutional grounds that he was a hound dog. The people knew Clinton was a hound dog and liked him anyhow, especially compared to "Newt" Gingrich, therefore this campaign failed.

Philadelphia Republicans nominated Bush in 2000. At that event, I met Moral Majority founder Jerry Falwell semi-intimately. We were guests of Tom Brokaw and Tim Russert on MSNBC from the convention hall. As previously stated in a piece, The Rev. Falwell came on the show to criticize gay people, whom he loves as Christians, as depraved perverts destined for hell. I have no idea why I was on the show. All I know is that when the Rev. Falwell finished his segment, a technician withdrew the earpiece from his ear and inserted the same heated earpiece into my ear with him standing next to me.

There was penetration. Earwax was likely exchanged. We didn't wear condoms, as far as I knew. But so what? Damn, it's 2000! Any two consenting male adults sharing an earpiece is their own business. I believe the Rev. Falwell shares this opinion, but I have not spoken to him. Please call me, Jerry! You big lug, I miss you!)

Los Angeles hosted the 2000 Democratic convention, where Al Gore was nominated. The Democrats had a sparkling galaxy of Hollywood stars at their convention, while the Republicans had Bo Derek.

During the convention, LA hosted glamorous, exclusive parties, but the press was not admitted. I got into one of the most exclusive parties, hosted by the influential lobbying firm Patton Boggs, which everyone was raving about. I entered by posing as the mayor's security detail with a group of cartoonists. Really.

My Los Angeles-based friend Ted Habte-Gabr caused this. Ted, a schmoozer, entrepreneur,53 cheerleader, and crazy, is the most outgoing person on Earth. He will ask for anything and generally gets it.

When I spoke at the University of Iowa in 1991, Ted, a student and lecture committee chair, was there. I was running for US president. I did this as a joke every four years since the early 1980s to write columns about it. I never campaigned, but I had bumper stickers created with slogans like:

DAVE BARRY FOR PRESIDENT
Yes, of the United States
DAVE BARRY FOR PRESIDENT
A Catchy Slogan Should Appear Here
DAVE BARRY FOR PRESIDENT
It's Time We Demanded Less

Ted called my Iowa speech a "State of the Union Address and Presidential Debate." Adam Nagourney, a serious political reporter for USA Today and the New York Times, covered me nationally. He told a semi-joking narrative about my campaign and joined me, Ted, and other students at Fitzpatrick's following my speech. Nagourney wrote in USA Today that he had four beers that night. I addressed the claim in a column, stating that I was followed to Iowa by a USA Today writer (motto: "If You Didn't Read It in USA Today, It Probably Contained More Than 50 Words"). He said I had four drinks at Fitzpatrick's and pledged to appoint every student in the bar to the US Supreme Court. This is another example of the media's obsession with sensationalized "dirt." I wish to clarify some "conveniently" left-out details from USA Today:

1. The USA Today reporter had AT LEAST three vodka–and–cranberry juices.
2. The Supreme Court might benefit greatly by the addition of several hundred college students. ("WASHINGTON—In a landmark decision yesterday, the Supreme Court ruled 356–9 that the Constitution contains WAY too many big words.")

Ted has been my campaign's field coordinator since I appointed him at Fitzpatrick's that evening. He has coordinated the field better than I have ran for president. He convinced Iowa farmer Daryl Neitderhiser to let me hold a baby pig for a photo op to show my support for agriculture. (Mr. Neitderhiser was worried I may infect his pig, making this difficult.)

Ted has also got several celebrities to pose with "Dave Barry for President" bumper stickers. At Ted's request, Kurt Vonnegut, Steve Allen, Frank McCourt, Barry White, Jules Feiffer, Robert Goulet, Jane Smiley, Steve Martin, Magic Johnson, Charlton Heston, Christopher Hitchens, Al Roker, Hugh Hefner, Donny Osmond, several Playboy Playmates, and Elmo have supported my candidacy (I have photos).

However, Richard "Dick" Riordan, a prominent Republican businessman, was Los Angeles mayor during the 2000 Democratic convention. Ted, my field coordinator, urged the mayor to endorse my presidential campaign when I was in LA covering the convention. Mayor Riordan, a quirky jokester, agreed.

So a meeting was planned. Mayor Riordan owns the Pantry, a famed Los Angeles coffee business. I was to join him for breakfast with my people. Unfortunately, I only had Ted. So I gathered cartoonists. I often hooked up with cartoonists at conventions because they were looking for ridiculous angles, too.

Mike Luckovich, Walt Handelsman, Dan Perkins, Rob Rogers, and Chip Bok—five Pulitzer Prize-winning cartoonists—accompanied me to the conference. After a delicious breakfast of fried cholesterol, the mayor endorsed me for president as promised. He then mentioned attending the elite Patton Boggs party that night. We instantly requested to be his security detail. We and his people were surprised when he answered yes.

At nine p.m., Ted, the cartoonists, and I met in the Sunset Room parking lot in Hollywood. We planned diligently for our mission:

- We wore dark suits (I bought mine that afternoon).
- We wore sunglasses, even though it was nighttime.
- For security purposes we had given ourselves Secret Code Names, including "Kitchen Magician," "Thrusting Rod" and "Pocket Fisherman." I was "Magenta Eagle."
- We had cords plugged into our ears. These were coiled cords that we had removed from our hotel telephones. We stuck the other end of the cord into our suits, connected to nothing. This was our communications system.

The mayor—our Secret Code Name "Sourdough"—and his wife ("Pork Chop") came last. The mayor had a real LAPD security detail, who didn't seem happy to see us.

We followed the mayor to the venue entrance, where Patton Boggs employees kept the riffraff out. They refused to acknowledge us. This was expected given we were fools wearing sunglasses at night and pretending to speak in code ("Pocket Fisherman, this is Magenta Eagle, do you copy?") into hotel phone cables in our ears. Before they could speak, Mayor Riordan—a once-in-a-generation leader—pointed to us and said, "They're with me." The gatekeepers had to allow us.

So we attended the pattonboggs party everyone was raving about. It was nothing special. It was great, but as usual with exclusive events, it was just people standing around.

Our assholery protected the Riordans for a while. Some distinguished-looking people—my faint recall is that they were from a foreign country, probably Spain—wanted to talk to the mayor, so we blocked their path and told them to keep back for security reasons. And they did!

Luckily, we discovered the open bar before we started an international crisis. We stayed throughout, allowing Sourdough and Pork Chop to secure themselves.

I thought that evening was the highlight of the 2000 presidential contest. The election, especially Florida's performance, was the lowpoint. Floridians couldn't figure out who they voted for. Was Bush George W? Al Gore? Perhaps William Shatner? We were unaware!

Florida election officials spent weeks examining ballots that appeared to have been attacked by rabid weasels to determine what voters were thinking, if "thinking" is the proper word. That election made Florida the Stupid State (Official motto: "Florida—You Can't Spell It Without Duh"). Florida has this reputation, but people keep relocating here from better states like New York that are supposed to stay above sea level, so go figure.

Bush triumphed. 9/11 and the Iraq War followed. The 2004 election focused on the War on Terror. It was anticipated that another major attack on US territory was impending, so we all took precautions like not boarding commercial flights with more than 3.4 ounces of shampoo. Still not doing this, but now we believe it's foolish.

The 2004 political conventions were mostly remembered for their paranoia and excessive security. Knight Ridder, which controlled the Miami Herald, required all reporters and photographers attending the conventions or Olympics (I did both) to take terrorism lessons. A pair of badass British paramilitary guys terrified the hell out of us by ordering us to flee away from a radioactive cloud or faint if a colleague was spitting blood from an essential artery.

We also received emergency supplies from Knight Ridder, as I wrote: I received an Anti-Terrorist Kit. Really. It includes a "evacuation hood" to cover your head during a gas assault, a lamp to temporarily blind terrorists, and a whistle to terrify them (or yourself if you blow it inside your hood).

I had trouble passing my Anti-Terrorist Kit past the Boston FleetCenter security checkpoint for the Democratic convention, even though we were ordered to carry it everywhere:

Three security personnel checked my kit. One held up the flashlight and asked me (swear) if it was a DNC-approved flashlight. They confiscated it when I stated I didn't know. How can I resist terrorism without a flashlight? Ha ha!" I joked in a jocular tone to show that I was a trained humorist, but the security guards were unamused, so I left before they took my whistle.

Like most of my coworkers, I left my Anti-Terrorist Kit in the hotel. We were spared by the terrorists, who were ignorant of our vulnerability.

Republicans renominated George W. Bush and Dick Cheney; Democrats nominated John Kerry and John Edwards. For a humorist, the Bush-Cheney ticket's second term was topped by Vice President Cheney's shotgun shot of a prominent attorney while hunting quail. Wikipedia says, "It was the first time someone had been shot by a sitting vice-president since Alexander Hamilton was shot in a duel by Aaron Burr in 1804."

Thankfully, the attorney recovered and the vice president was not charged. I wrote in my 2006 Year in Review that "Local authorities ruled the shooting was an accident, noting that if the vice president were going to intentionally shoot somebody, it would be Nancy Pelosi."

The 2008 presidential contest was about change after eight years of Bush-Cheney. I wrote from New Hampshire that all candidates, Democrat and Republican, are now for change. They're getting more enthusiastic about Change every day; they'll soon demand for tactical air strikes on Washington.

The Democratic party's big news was that Barack Obama was suddenly seriously challenging Hillary Clinton, who had been heavily predicted to win the nomination. While in New Hampshire, Obama's rallies drew large crowds. As I wrote, I headed to Derry to attend a crowded rally for the rising presidential candidate. People cheered, chanted, and threw underpants at him. Those were journalists.

I kid! In some way.

Obama said he was for change before it was cool. He remains committed to change. He made repeated subtle references to "my opponent, the screeching harpy," but did not identify Hillary Clinton.

I kid! In some way.

When the Democrats met in Denver to nominate Obama-Biden, the Obama-Clinton rivalry was still bitter:

Occasionally, Obama and Clinton delegates have fired. Political watchers believe this indicates ongoing friction between the two parties. Clinton has publicly urged her supporters to work for Obama, but one Obama official called her use "a lot of air quotes."

Being resentful is hard to blame on Sen. Clinton. Here she is, the smartest person ever, PLUS she spent all those years standing loyally behind Bill Clinton wearing uncomfortable pantyhose (Hillary was, not Bill) (although there are rumors), PLUS she went to the trouble and expense of acquiring a legal residence in New York State so she could be a senator, PLUS she assembled a team of nuclear-physicist-grade genius political advisors, PLUS she spent years going around to every dirtbag community After that, she loses the nomination to a guy with similar executive government experience as Hannah Montana. Hillary asks, "Are you KIDDING me?"

John McCain, the Republican nominee, surprised the political world by choosing Alaska governor Sarah Palin as his running mate. She was the focus of talk at the St. Paul Republican meeting:

After growing tired of Sarah Palin speculation and gossip, the news media is finally focusing on more of it as the Republican convention winds down and John McCain prepares to give his acceptance speech. All anybody talks about at this convention is this. Palin-Palooza. Critics wonder how much McCain knew about Palin before he chose her as his running mate, especially because he calls her "whatshername" in speeches. McCain's crew claims it investigated

Palin thoroughly, including scrutinizing her driver's license and "reading almost her entire Wikipedia article."

Questions persist. Reporters are scouring Wasilla, Alaska, for Palin's past. The lessons learned so far:

Luxury hotels are few in Wasilla.

Same with eateries.

Obama-Biden handily won the general election, therefore on Inauguration Day, January 20, 2009, two historic occurrences happened:

Barack Obama was our first Black president.

I joined his inaugural parade.

Yes. This is me, a member of the World Famous Lawn Rangers, an exclusive marching company that only accepts applicants. Arcola, a small central Illinois town that proudly calls itself the Broomcorn Capital of the World because it once produced lots of corn used to create old-fashioned brooms, is home to the Rangers, who conduct precision parade maneuvers with lawnmowers and brooms. Arcola hosts the Broomcorn Festival in September, featuring a parade with the World Famous Lawn Rangers.

As a professional comedy journalist, I had to accept Pat Monahan's 1992 invitation to march with the Rangers in the parade. To hide my identity, I went to Arcola and got a broom, lawnmower, cowboy hat, and black Lone Ranger mask. During Rookie Orientation, I learned the Rangers' two precision marching maneuvers: "Walk the Dog," where you push your mower in a clockwise circle while holding your broom aloft, and "Cross and Toss," where you exchange sides and toss your brooms to each other.

That first parade, marching down Arcola's main street with my fellow Rangers, pushing our mowers, doing our maneuvers, and seeing the crowd's reactions, some of whom were so awed by our superb perfection they could hardly stand, will never leave me. Since then, I've marched in Broomcorn parades as a proud Ranger.

Rangers will march in any procession that has them. They met a promising young US Senate candidate in 2003 while walking in

Chicago's St. Patrick's Day parade. You guessed it—that politician was Abraham Lincoln.

It was Barack Obama. He smiles enthusiastically and triumphantly holds a toilet plunger in a Rangers photo. (When the Rangers march, column leaders use toilet plungers to signal our precision maneuver.)

Pat Monahan remembered that shot and applied to the inauguration organizers to have the Rangers march in the parade in 2008. I told him he was crazy when he said this. Traditional inaugural parades have highly disciplined military groups and musicians that prepare for hours, wear identical uniforms, and rarely have to urinate mid-parade due to beer overconsumption. No doubt, Pat, the Rangers would not march.

I was mistaken. Maybe parade organizers wanted to be funny. Perhaps they were broom industry fans. For some reason, the Rangers were accepted.

On that frigid January day in Washington, with night falling, fifty-six Lawn Rangers walked the parade route with brooms and pushed lawnmowers trucked in from Arcola, one of which had the Obama plunger portrait. We were freezing after hours of waiting. I described the scene in a column:

By night, the parade crowd is mostly police officers controlling the nonexistent crowd. We showed our two precision lawnmower techniques. After not practicing, our first few attempts are rusty, but the viewers are impressed, as shown by their laughs.

As we walk up Pennsylvania Avenue, the crowd grows, yet we can still see everyone. My column partner, Bernie Casella, occasionally exclaims, "Thanks for coming!"

A brightly lit street awaits us around the corner. In front of the White House are reviewing stands and a presidential party enclosure. Finished.

As we push our mowers ahead with fresh zest, they appear, staring at us from a few feet away: Barack and Michelle Obama, and Joe Biden. The president points to the mower with his plunger photo and addresses the First Lady. They're laughing. Whew.

Our precision lawnmower maneuver benefits the presidential party. After a few seconds, we return to the darkness and cold.

However, we feel good. Because tonight we made a statement. Our position is that an inauguration is a serious event, but it is also a time to celebrate the diversity of this wonderful nation, including clowns.

President appeared to understand: Sir, on behalf of all the Rangers, we wish you the best in approaching your many massive tasks. If you march with us again, we'll reheat your plunger.

Obama, for whatever reason, did not march with the Lawn Rangers after being elected president. Even though Mitt Romney was his Republican opponent, Democrats renominated him in 2012.

In a Tampa GOP convention essay, I noticed Romney's main issue was seeming accessible to everyday people:

The Republican convention opened Tuesday with a parade of speakers proclaiming the evening's theme, "Mitt Romney: You're Darned Tooting He's Human!"

The Republicans believe Mitt's biggest issue is that many voters don't perceive a regular person like them. This tall, fit, handsome, rich Mormon with a square jaw and perfect hair, a blond wife, and at least 23 tall, handsome clone sons appears calculating and reserved. He has never gotten hammered and danced the Funky Chicken at a wedding reception and passed out face-down in the prime rib.

Voters notice this and think, "This man can't possibly relate to me and my everyday problems, such as my financial woes, my hemorrhoids, and this tendency I have to talk to myself."

The Republicans paraded humanizers, led by Mitt's wife Ann. She movingly described a Mitt Romney most people have never seen: witty, spontaneous, tender, laid-back, five feet tall, overweight, bald, and Jewish in some places.

Romney lost to Obama despite his wife's endorsement. That was the last election without much controversy, compared to what followed.

The 2016 election showed that smart, well-educated, well-credentialed people—who feel themselves more informed than the average citizen—sometimes don't know what's going on. My profession, journalism, has many such folks.

I dined with journalists and politicians at the 2016 Republican convention. Although it was a private, off-the-record gathering, I can assure you that this was a distinguished collection of famous, successful, and respected people. They were positive Hillary Clinton will beat Donald Trump in the general election. All politicians knew this.

Definitely knew it. I mocked Trump in books and columns for decades. I mocked his presidential ambitions in 1999, when he came to Miami to consider a run. Trump, who calls himself "the very definition of the American success story," visited Miami on Monday to gauge his popularity. I published a column on my observations. He arrived at Miami International Airport (motto: "You Expect to Get Your Luggage BACK?") shortly after 10 a.m. in a private 727 airplane with enormous, shiny gold letters spelling out "RYDER."

Actually, they spelled "TRUMP," which appears on Trump's casinos, hotels, condominiums, ex-wives, etc. Several Trump employees, a UPS truck-looking bodyguard, and Melania Knauss, the official Trump girlfriend and supermodel, were on the Trump plane.

The Bay of Pigs veterans library and memorial in Little Havana was the next stop for Trump and his entourage, who motorcaded with police. Trump told the packed audience that "Fidel Castro actually has done some good things."

I'm kidding again. Castro is horrible, he said. This boldness won over the crowd.

Everyone then motorcaded to the Radisson Mart Plaza Hotel for a news conference, where Trump candidly stated, "I've done very well at everything I've ever done." Having looked at Al Gore and George W. Bush, he was unimpressed.

His phrase, "Let me ask you," is authentic. "Did they make billions quickly? No. Could they make billions quickly? I disagree."

Very hard to argue with that. Too long, losers have run our country who have never made a billion dollars quickly. One example is Abraham Lincoln.

That was one of several essays I've written about Trump's idiocy over the years. So in 2016, I and all the clever people thought his campaign was a farce. Everyone expected Hillary Clinton to win.

That premise was flawed because Democrats were not cohesive. Clinton struggled to defeat Bernie Sanders in a heated Democratic nomination campaign. At the Democratic convention in Philadelphia, Clinton and Sanders delegates seemed to detest each other more than Trump. My opening session piece covered this:

The Democratic convention gaveled and Boyz II Men performed well, but then there was a significant split. This happened during the invocation. The Rev. Cynthia Hale basically asked God to bless the Democratic Party. It was OK until she uttered "Hillary Rodham Clinton."

The hall erupted with Bernie Sanders delegates shouting "BERNIE!" and Clinton delegates shouting "HILLARY!" It was so noisy that the Rev. Hale was unable to speak to God, who had likely probably watched the Republican convention and was rolling His eyes and considering going third party or perhaps creating a new planet.

The Rev. Hale finished the invocation, and the Pledge of Allegiance went well because it didn't mention Hillary Clinton.

Disunity persisted throughout the day, but by evening it had subsided. Sanders, the night's most anticipated speaker, heartfeltly urged his supporters to back Clinton because "otherwise they will shoot my dog."

Sanders gave Clinton a solid support. He did so with a pained grimace, but he always does. He looks like a box turtle passing a kidney stone even when he's happy.

Cleveland hosted the Republican convention. As I noted in my first column from there, many high-level Republicans who expected Trump to lose did not attend:

As the phrase goes, "You can't spell 'fun' without using some of the letters in 'Republican.'" The GOP convention is in town, and the whole crew is here, so Cleveland is in for a blast!

Not the whole crew. Much of the Republican Party had to leave the convention at the last minute because of a haircut appointment. Arthur A. "Bud" Klampf, deputy vice mayor of Ant Mound, Arkansas, is the highest-ranking Republican elected official here and will give "a major prime-time address, assuming he can locate his dentures."

The excitement will peak on Tuesday, when the Republican delegates, barring a last-minute commando assault led by George Will in a camouflage bow tie, are expected to nominate Donald J. Trump, who according to recent polls has a chance to defeat Hillary Clinton and become president. Are you serious?

Oops! I dropped my professional-journalism objectivity mask. Professional journalists are panicking because no matter how hard we attempt to convince the public that Trump is unqualified, many people still like him and his daring vision for America, which is whatever comes to mind at the moment. Journalists ask, "What's wrong with you?" Why are you NOT listening?! Our Twitter accounts are verified! We're professional journalists.

Sorry, I needed to vent.

In that column, I joked about Trump's prospects of winning—I didn't think he had any—but not about the media's subjectiveness. Many know reporters are more liberal than conservative. Regardless of their views, the political reporters I've worked with over the years have attempted to be objective and professional. I thought mainstream media covered politics fairly. Until Trump.

For the record, I hate Trump. This narcissistic jerk and liar behaved horribly on January 6. I'd never vote for him.

But I don't think anyone can disagree that the large papers and networks were anti-Trump in huge and minor ways.

Some of my colleagues argue that we journalists should abandon our neutrality because Trump is uniquely corrupt and dangerous, an existential threat of Hitlerian proportions.

The issue with this reasoning is that when the public sees us choosing sides—and they do—we lose our credibility, which was our only influence. We become another basement blogger and partisan voice in a cacophonous chorus.

As I write, public trust in the media is horribly low. Too many people no longer trust us to be honest. I hate to say it, but we may not win them back. We won't win them back by saying the problem isn't our blunders but that people are too foolish to agree with us.

I have clever, respected friends that think I'm wrong about this problem. They believe the media has been too accommodating of Trump, allowing him to get away with dishonesty that would not be permitted from any other leader.

Maybe I'm mistaken. No, I disagree. But possibly.

Trump won the 2016 election, and politics has been a mess since. I haven't campaigned since then, partly because of COVID-19, partly because I'm old, and partly because it's less fun.

Fun aside: This chapter is excessively serious. Move on to brighter topics.

CHAPTER 7
BOOKS, MUSIC AND MOVIES

Shirley Wood, a Los Angeles woman, called me unexpectedly in June 1984. She said she was a talent supervisor for The Tonight Show and was considering scheduling me to be interviewed by JOHNNY FREAKING CARSON.

She didn't shout in capital letters, but my brain did. The 1984 Carson show was tremendous. Everything watched, and all the great stars were visitors. A Tonight Show appearance might launch a comedian's career.

Carson occasionally hosted authors, generally bestsellers like Truman Capote. I had two novels and a very little name. Bad Habits, a collection of my early newspaper essays, reached my mom's nationwide readership. The Taming of the Screw, a 1983 Rodale Press paperback, was my second book. It was a satire of bad DIY home improvement guides. I said the easiest method to unclog a toilet was to shoot it. I wanted to call the book Shoot Your Toilet, but Rodale Press thought it was too crass.

I appeared on one Philadelphia TV morning talk show to promote The Taming of the Screw. This appearance did not boost sales. It appeared nobody watched. Not sure the cameraman saw it. However, Shirley Wood acquired a tape of that appearance about a year later. She auditioned me by phone, asking book questions and listening to my amusing answers. After my answers, she said "No" or "OK." Not once did she chuckle. However, she booked me on Tonight.

That was my second TV appearance. From a local show nobody watched to a national show millions watched. The Tonight Show flew me from Philadelphia to Los Angeles and picked me up in a limo—I had never been in one—to the studio, where I was shown a dressing room with my name on it. I wasn't dressed—I'd flown in my show clothes—so I sat in my dressing room apprehensive until Shirley Wood came in and went over Carson's questions. She then took me to the backstage bar and gave me a long glass of wine, which I drank. Still anxious, I stood for an hour. I then appeared on The Tonight Show.

It worked. Listen up—Johnny Carson was a great interviewer. After my experience, everyone asked me, "What's Carson like?" I mean, how would I know? In the seven minutes I sat next to him on national television, he never leant over to tell me about himself. However, he was really professional. He prepared me for all the jokes and let me laugh. It didn't bother him when I interrupted his inquiries in my excitement to answer. He could have replied, "Dave, I know that you know these questions, inasmuch as you and Shirley Wood discussed them for an hour today, but it's conceivable that some members of the audience may not know them." But he didn't. After the first minute, I knew I was in good hands and would be alright. By the conclusion of the show, I was enjoying myself till I was sick on Dick Cavett.

I didn't vomit on Dick Cavett—that was a prank. I sat between him and Johnny Carson, so I could have. Carson even laughed about my book's premise in a quiet time. After the section ended and the red camera light went off, he lit a cigarette, turned to me, and said, "I used to try to do it yourself. [Pause.] Can't do shit yourself."

Within three hours, I was seated in the coach section of a red-eye aircraft back to Philadelphia, totally awake, surrounded by napping non-celebrities who were clueless that I had just been interviewed by JOHNNY FREAKING CARSON

That interview was widely viewed, selling books and opening opportunities. Not all were suitable doors. A nice Cape Cod hardware business owner couple contacted me. My Carson impression was amazing, so they invited me to autograph books at their store. They loved this idea. My book was about home repair, so they thought hardware-store consumers would like it. It fit perfectly! I'd sell many books! If I paid for my transportation up there, they'd cover half of the lodging!

This sounded like a good strategy to me—probably because I was stupid. I drove to Cape Cod, which is far from suburban Philadelphia, on Friday and held an event at the pleasant couple's hardware store on Saturday. They had ordered over 100 copies of my book and posted a notice in the store front promoting my arrival. I was supposed to stay four hours.

I think I sold five books, if I remember correctly. It may have been less. Hardware shopping is the main reason consumers visit hardware stores. Even if the author has appeared on national TV, they're not interested in a comedic book.

When people entered the store, the charming couple would pull them over to me and tell them how funny I was on Carson and that I sold books. After this revelation, there was several seconds of awkward stillness, which is when people are trying to leave without buying your book.

After this agonizing experience multiple times, I urged the wonderful couple to stop trying to sell my book to random customers. I poked around the store for four hours looking at hardware. I became knowledgeable enough with the stock to help customers who mistook me for an employee (which happened multiple times) get what they needed.

For most authors other than Stephen King, author celebrity is like that. Being interviewed by Johnny Carson might make you feel famous. As this list shows, authors are often reminded how low they rank in the celebrity ecosystem:

Top 30 Celebrity Occupations
1. Taylor Swift
2. Major movie star such as Tom Cruise
3. Musical superstar other than Taylor Swift
4. Star athlete
5. Kardashian
6. President of the United States
7. Major TV star
8. Elon Musk
9. Whoever is currently dating Taylor Swift
10. Stephen King

11. Celebrity DJ
12. Major Internet influencer you've never heard of but your kids have
13. Supermodel
14. (Tie) The GEICO Gecko and "Flo" of Progressive Insurance
15. Celebrity chef
16. Celebrity fashion designer
17. Celebrity billionaire other than Elon Musk
18. Person doing some idiot thing in a viral video
19. The Pope
20. Stand-up comedian with a Netflix special
21. Member of the British royal family
22. "Reality" TV show star
23. The Dalai Lama
24. Minor movie star such as that guy, whatshisname, in that movie
25. Whoever was previously dating Taylor Swift
26. Vice president of the United States
27. TV weatherperson
28. Nobel Prize winner
29. Author other than Stephen King
30. Member of Congress

Authors are the least famous celebrity after Congress. The book industry is minor compared to other popular diversions like professional cornhole.

How little? Look at the numbers. Making one of the New York Times bestseller lists is huge in the book industry. A book that just makes it to the bottom of a list and stays there for a week will always be called a New York Times bestseller. Because several of my books are in that category.

Guess how many copies a book must sell in a week to be on the Times list. Anyway, a thousand books, give or take. Your book could be a New York Times bestseller if the number of people worldwide who buy your book is somewhat fewer than the average attendance at a Modesto Nuts game in a given week.

Every book you sell counts. Most authors spend a lot of time and energy promoting their novels in stores. This is why they hold book-signings in bookstores or, if they're stupid, hardware stores, despite the danger of few or no customers attending. This is why authors obsessively check their Amazon rankings and get pleased when their book rises from 63,981 to 47,828. Fair enough, some authors never check Amazon ranks. Authors lie to sell their books, leading them to go on book tours. At least I did.

An Oprah Winfrey Show producer called me in 1996 while I was in St. Louis on a book tour. Oprah sold a lot of books, so this call was as exciting as the Tonight Show call. Any book she chose for her book club was a hit. Oprah's club only examined serious, meaningful novels without booger jokes, not mine. But having Oprah mention a book on her broadcast was enormous for an author.

The producer wanted me on a show's guest panel the next day. Show theme: "Things We Do in Secret." We guests would admit our mistakes and repair them on air. The producer wanted to know what I could disclose.

Of course I agreed. I would have claimed sole responsibility for the JFK assassination to go on Oprah. But I came up with theft. Years previously, I slept at a Hyatt with a plastic restroom sign that read:

Our towels are 100 percent cotton. Should you wish to purchase a set, they are available in the gift store. Should you prefer the set in your bathroom, a $75 charge will automatically be added to your bill.

Hyatt politely stated: If you steal our towels, you'll pay $75.

I stole the sign. It entertained guests in our guest bathroom for years after I brought it home.

One Oprah producer stated my tale was perfect. She suggested I tell my tale on radio and drop the sign into a "give-back" box where they collected stolen items. The producer stated returning the sign was "essential" on air.

"OK!" I said. "No problem!"

Unfortunately, I was in St. Louis, the event was in Chicago the next day, and the sign was in Miami. I called Michelle and instructed her to FedEx the sign to Chicago as fast as possible, but I wasn't sure it would arrive in time. I doubted I'd be on Oprah if not. This concerned me much.

Then I realized: My St. Louis Hyatt room had a plastic sign. The hotel's no-smoking policy was explained here, although it was hard to detect.

I stole that sign.

The original sign arrived in Chicago on schedule, and Oprah and her studio audience approved when I returned it on air. I was willing to steal and deceive again to appear in a show about righting past wrongs. To Oprah!

On a book tour, you must. I appeared on Bill Maher's Politically Incorrect show several times to debate major issues. The commitment to mention my books was my only motive for going on those shows. I have no expertise or strong opinions about the problems we discussed. Despite not caring much about the issues, I debated them fiercely. I fought with panelists. I got so into it with Vicki Lawrence, the actress and comedienne from The Carol Burnett Show who sang "The Night the Lights Went Out in Georgia," that she rose to her feet and raged at me for something I said about the death sentence. I had a heated argument with Micky Dolenz on another Politically Incorrect. I don't recall what, but I felt firmly that as an author promoting a book, I had to speak up for my values.

Book tours generally involve promoting the book. In several interviews, you repeat the same words to sound enthusiastic, even when you're starting to loathe your book.

Your interviewers may have read your book, but rarely. Not necessarily their fault. They don't have time to read your book on a morning-drive radio show with music, traffic, and weather or a local TV news broadcast with nineteen other features. Sometimes they have no time to discuss your book. Many interviews with noon TV-news anchors went like this:

ANCHORPERSON: With us now is humor author Dave Barry, who has a new book. Welcome, Dave!

ME: Thank you!

CO-ANCHORPERSON: So, Dave, what's this book about?

ME: Computers.

CO-ANCHORPERSON: Ha ha!

ANCHORPERSON: Funny stuff! Thank you, Dave Barry! On a more tragic note, a kennel fire has claimed the lives of fifty-three puppies. For more on that story, we go to...

All authors recall embarrassing book-tour interviews. Late historian David McCullough recounted my favorite. He was interviewed on TV about his Panama Canal book, The Path Between the Seas, and the host asked him about the US giving Panama the canal. David replied that, "like Normandy Beach," the canal would always belong to the US regardless of its legal status.

David said the interviewer seemed confused, paused, and added, "I don't understand. Norman D. Beach—who?"

Meeting readers, who instead of staying home and watching TV, go to bookstores to see you, pay for your books, wait in line to sign them, and nearly always act like you're helping them, is the best part of book tours. They sometimes bring gifts. T-shirts, whoopee cushions, cakes, cookies, Pop-Tarts, Pez dispensers, a coconut brassiere, beer—a lot of beer—Slim Jims, Cheez-Its, regular brownies, and highly irregular brownies have been delivered to me by my readers.

How many thousands of volumes have I autographed in forty years of book touring? I've autographed other authors' books, photos, newspaper clippings, CDs, tapes, Kindles, computers, clothes, caps, shoes, casts, arms, legs, chests, foreheads, and several babies' diapers. People usually ask me to personalize books for them or others. Sometimes they want me to write a special note like "Happy Birthday!", "Keep laughing!", or "You're an idiot!" for the book recipient. They sometimes want me to write inspiring messages like "Keep striving and you will achieve your dreams!" something I would never say.

I'll write almost whatever clients request. The book is theirs. I may put "For [name], with best wishes" or some false message like "For [name], my closest personal friend" if they don't care.

Dedicated to my idol, [name], without whom I would not have created this book.

During my time as a mother, I enjoyed meeting readers and still do. Social media and virtual events are replacing multicity book tours. Books have rarely sold well on book tours. Word-of-mouth from women sells books.

Woman read more books, especially novels, than men. Women are also better at expressing their thoughts than guys, who are frequently reluctant to declare how they feel about anything other than pass interference. Women tell others they like a book. Books become bestsellers that way.

Witnessed this process firsthand. Remember Khaled Hosseini's bestseller The Kite Runner? That book sold seven million copies, and I believe five million was due to pressure from my wife, Michelle, a woman. For a year after reading The Kite Runner, she suggested that everyone she met—in bookstores, on flights, in elevators and public restrooms, on Disney World's Small World ride—buy it.

True story: Sophie's preschool class enjoyed a Mother's Day lunch when she was four. The teachers requested the kids to describe their mothers and wrote them on wall posters. Other moms' posters included, "My mom bakes cookies," "My mom plays with me," and "My mom is pretty." I didn't set Sophie up to say this, but Michelle's poster said, "My mom tells everyone to read The Kite Runner."

I met Khaled Hosseini. A lovely guy and a good writer. To my knowledge, he is not married to my wife. Since I am. I often asked Michelle if she could make one of my novels a bestseller if she had a few minutes during her yearlong advertising campaign for The Kite Runner. She giggled and told me she likes my novels each time. She promoted The Kite Runner again.

Many of my novels have done well without my wife's help. Two of them were successful enough for a TV producer to get the rights to use them as the basis for the early 1990s CBS sitcom Dave's World. It starred late Harry Anderson as newspaper columnist Dave Barry.

That was strange because many people thought I wrote the show and that it reflected my life. Neither supposition was right. Los Angeles-based TV writers wrote the show, which featured Dave getting into crazy comedic situations with his family, friends, and coworkers like Miami Record-Dispatch editor Kenny Beckett (Shadoe Stevens). Dave learned life lessons at the end of many episodes.

My life was different. I spent hours and days staring at a computer screen in a room with two dogs and no other people, thinking: This is not amusing. The only life lesson I learned was that dogs fart a lot. My real newspaper was the Miami Herald, and my editor was Tom Shroder, who was more competent than Shadoe Stevens but had less hair.

I don't mean to complain. The Dave's World staff was always kind and paid me for book rights. The first season, they flew me to California to meet everyone and make a cameo. Two men competed to buy the remaining air conditioner in an appliance store during a heat wave. Harry Anderson played me, and I was a terrible actor.

Harry was humorous, smart, and unpretentious, so I enjoyed hanging around with him. He knew I'd performed in rock bands, so he suggested we do "Wild Thing" on guitars at the end of the episode. Never played guitar, Harry. He practiced the chords for 15 minutes, but "Wild Thing" requires more.

Harry and I play a verse and chorus on guitar during the episode's end credits. I stop playing and exclaim, "Take it!" Harry plays the worst solo of "Wild Thing" ever. I stop him after ten seconds and say, "OK, give it back."

That was fun. However, I was pleased when Dave's World ended because it was strange having a network TV show about a guy with my name living a life that was technically mine but wasn't.

A few years after Dave's World, I wrote my first novel. Tom Shroder's concept sparked this. He wanted to showcase South Florida writers, so he asked thirteen of us to work on a serial story published weekly in the Herald's Sunday Tropic magazine. We each wrote a chapter and passed it on.

I composed the first chapter on Booger, a manatee. Elmore "Dutch" Leonard authored the second-to-last chapter, and Carl Hiaasen bravely finished it. We named it Naked Came the Manatee after Newsday journalists' 1969 satirical sex novel Naked Came the Stranger.

Naked Came the Manatee was poor writing. The scenario involved two severed heads, reportedly belonging to Fidel Castro, and was complicated and unlikely. The story also showed Booger becoming more forceful and clever, unlike most manatees, and performing heroic deeds like a big fat aquatic Lassie.

However, Tropic readers appreciated the project, and to our surprise, Neil Nyren, Carl Hiaasen's Putnam editor, bought it and published it as a book. Because Carl, Dutch, and I didn't have to take it seriously, our week in New York doing publicity was the most fun I've ever had marketing a book.

The best was on Charlie Rose, when Rose asked Dutch, "Have you read this book?" after Dutch gave imprecise responses. Dutch, Carl, and I laughed uncontrollably since Dutch hadn't read the book. His research assistant had given him enough information to write a separate chapter, so he gave Carl entire storyline responsibility. Dutch Leonard was no idiot.

Even so, Naked Came the Manatee sold well (all revenues went to charity). Neil Nyren enjoyed my first chapter and asked if I wanted to write a novel. Before that, I never considered writing novels. I considered myself a joke writer. My columns and books were joke collections. I never wrote a plot.

I wrote Big Trouble because Neil was paying me to try. Municipal corruption, Russian gangsters selling Soviet military equipment from a Miami bar, a runaway herd of Santeria sacrifice goats, and toad-secreted psychedelics were story components. I wish I could say these elements sprang from my fertile imagination, but they all came from Miami Herald news pieces.

Big Trouble debuted in 1999. It received positive reviews and became a New York Times bestseller (not Modesto Nuts). First-time novelists dream of seeing their work produced into a movie, but mine had an unexpected twist.

The film was expensive and studio-backed. Barry Sonnenfeld directed it and starred Tim Allen, Rene Russo, Sofia Vergara, Stanley Tucci, Zooey Deschanel, Omar Epps, Dennis Farina, Ben Foster, Janeane Garofalo, Johnny Knoxville, Jason Lee, Heavy D, Tom Sizemore, and Patrick Warburton. The screenplay was written Robert Ramsey and Matthew Stone.

The filming in Miami was surreal—watching my words become movie sets at great cost. I wrote a treehouse scene in the novel. An army of movie crews descended with a fleet of cars and lots of equipment on an unsuspecting tree for several lengthy, intense, and often frantic days to film that scene. Similar to Normandy, but with better food.

This was simply one scene in the movie, which lasts around two minutes. This happened throughout Miami in summer and fall 2000. The crew spent a week on a Miami International Airport concourse filming a scene in which two unskilled crooks board an airline with a suitcase they think holds jewels but really carries a nuclear explosive. The studio spent $40 million on Big Trouble and $6 million promoting it. I attended the Miami advance screening with my family and friends before the Hollywood debut. I was excited to sleep that night.

Michelle immediately called me the next morning to come see the TV. September 11, 2001.

Not a good time to release a silly cinematic comedy with an airborne suitcase bomb.

The Big Trouble release was delayed. A low-key Hollywood premiere and limited advertising before its April 2002 release. It was poorly received and left cinemas swiftly. It flopped at the box office, but TV replays made it a cult favorite. Some find it quite good.

I believe it's fine, yet 9/11 comes to mind. Though unreasonable, this feeling makes the movie less enjoyable. After its 2002 premiere, I didn't watch it again until I showed it in St. Petersburg, Russia, twelve years later. I'll backtrack to describe how that happened because it includes my buddy and sometime partner Ridley Pearson.

In 1992, Kathi Goldmark created the Rock Bottom Remainders, an author rock band, where I met Ridley. In addition to Ridley and me, the band has had Mitch Albom, Sam Barry, Tad Bartimus, Roy Blount Jr., Robert Fulghum, Matt Groening, Carl Hiaasen, Greg Iles, Mary Karr, Stephen King, Barbara Kingsolver, Greil Marcus, Dave Marsh, James McBride, Frank McCourt, Joel Selvin, Amy Tan, Scott Turow, and Alan Zweibel.

These writers excel. Some are talented musicians. Remainders are a bad band. We hardly qualify as mediocre. Roy Blount called our music "hard-listening music." Our T-shirts proclaimed, "This Band Plays Music as Well as Metallica Writes Novels."

I admit it—being in the Remainders has been one of my life highlights. I love hanging out with fellow authors, talking about everything except writing, and making fools of ourselves onstage. But I also adore producing music with others, however poorly, and I'd missed that since Federal Duck.

Despite our shortcomings, we've played with some amazing musicians, starting with rock superstar Al Kooper, who bravely became our musical director early on. He gave us a pep talk after our first rehearsal: "When we started this morning, we stunk. Our stench improved by afternoon. Maybe we can become a faint odor."

Roger McGuinn, another rock classic, has played with the Remainders off and on for years. He makes us sound like the Byrds, especially when we turn our amps down. The late Warren Zevon, a Carl Hiaasen friend, liked playing with the Remainders and joined us several times. Lesley Gore sang "It's My Party" with us. We backed Judy Collins on "Both Sides Now," Darlene Love on "He's a Rebel," and Gloria Gaynor on "I Will Survive."

We played a bookstore convention in Los Angeles in 1994. We learned that a special guest was in the house and eager to join us onstage as we finished our last song. We allowed Bruce Springsteen play even though he wasn't an author.

He walked out in jeans, T-shirt, and baseball cap, and everyone went crazy. I gave him my guitar, assuring that I could always say I possessed a Bruce Springsteen guitar. Finally, we sang "Gloria."

Yes, I sing lead on that song. In the chorus, I spell "G-L-O-R-I-A!" while the backup singers say "GLOOOOR-I-A!" If you don't understand, Bruce Springsteen sang backing for me. His career took off then.

The Remainders have given me many great moments. My favorite part of the band is the friendships. Returning to Ridley Pearson. He and I clicked immediately. Bassist and musician extraordinaire. I always stand close to him since he knows technical details like what song we should play.

So Ridley and I became good friends and coauthors in 2004. Ridley was reading Peter Pan to his daughter Paige when she stopped him and asked: How did Peter Pan meet Captain Hook? Ridley thought the question was great and the answer could be a book. He asked me to collaborate on a Peter Pan prequel. I agreed because it seemed like a short, pleasant activity.

It was fun. It was neither fast nor small. For the following six years, it dominated my writing. We planned a simple children's book but wrote Peter and the Starcatchers, a 450-page YA novel. It excelled. The Broadway play Peter and the Starcatcher (without the final "s"), adapted by Rick Elice, won five Tony awards.

Disney published Peter and the Starcatchers, so Ridley and I had Disney-themed promotions. For a huge book signing at Walt Disney World Contemporary Resort, they built a replica pirate ship with a working cannon. Disney characters as Peter Pan and Captain Hook were present.

Ridley, I, and Peter Pan spent 15 minutes in a little room together while waiting for the event to start. Being a Disney cast member in costume meant he had to stay in character, which was awkward. I tried to chat with him before learning about this policy. The outcome was poor.

ME: So how do you work at Disney?

PETER PAN (placing hands on hips): It's a beautiful day in Never Land!

ME: Huh.

(Fifteen seconds of awkward silence)

PETER PAN: Have you seen Wendy?

If you want to experience a long fifteen minutes, try hanging out in a small confined space with Peter Pan.

Ridley and I wound up writing five books in the Starcatchers series. We also wrote a standalone YA novel called Science Fair, which resulted in one of my favorite fan letters ever, from two elementary-school boys:

Dear Mr. Barry and Mr. Pearson:

We both think your book "Science Fair" is one of the awesomest books out there. Just to warn you, two authors that our book club has written to have died. We hope the curse passes you by so you can make a sequel as soon as possible.

Sincerely,

[Names]

P.S. for most of the letter we alternated writing three words at a time.

Ridley and I went on many book tours, but Russia was our favorite in 2014. We were part of the US State Department's American Writers Series, which sends authors there to enhance relations. The US and Russia are almost at war, hence this scheme failed. But I don't deserve blame. Ridley was to blame.

However, Ridley and I did our best there despite difficult conditions. For me, "challenging circumstances" means "a world-class case of the trots."

On our second night in Moscow, I foolishly ate at a Mexican restaurant, which you should never do in Russia. Russians who don't like Mexican food ran it. (Honestly, they're not great at Russian food either.)

I think I ate a weaponized chimichanga at this Russian Mexican eatery. I developed a serious case of CBS, or Chernobyl Bowel Syndrome, from this, so we should all pray that the Russians never release it.

Besides that, I enjoyed exploring Russia, at least where bathrooms were within sprinting distance. Ridley and I gave many Russian lectures on our careers and how we wrote Starcatchers. The slide show includes a photo of me embarrassing my son Rob by picking him up at his middle school in the Oscar Mayer Wienermobile when I was a newspaper columnist.

This photo—they don't have the Wienermobile there—made Russian audiences wonder how we lost the Cold War to these people.

Most groups we spoke to were pleasant and receptive. I asked them what stereotypes Americans had of Russians after each session. They naturally mentioned two inaccurate stereotypes: that they all drink vodka and are thugs.

Finally, back to Big Trouble, which may have triggered this detour regarding my acquaintance with Ridley (though I doubt it). The American consulate in St. Petersburg requested me to perform a special event after our Russia tour. Monthly cinema nights in the consul general's home invited Russians to see American films. After seeing my novel converted into a movie, they decided it would be interesting to show Big Trouble and have me promote it.

I examined the plot on screening day to prepare my introduction as I hadn't watched the film since the 2002 debut. I had the challenge of introducing a movie with Russian characters, who are often stereotyped as gangsters, to an audience of Russians who are offended by this caricature.

That was a lot of fun—not fun. I mentioned in my opening that Big Trouble's Russian characters were clever criminals, unlike many of the American characters, who were both criminal and stupid. I doubt this calmed the audience. The American Writers Series program's goal was to improve relations between the US and Russia, but I may have contributed to our near-war. My sincerest apologies.

I had another cinematic career adventure shortly after Big Trouble. It started with this email:

Hi Dave, it's Steve Martin.

I'm hosting the Oscars this year [2003] and am trying to put together a team of geniuses to help me write it. Here's my question: do you know any? HA!

I'm wondering if the idea appeals to you at all. You, me, Rita Rudner and a few others. Best Oscar monologue ever. California. Tickets to the show. Fame.

I know you won't do it, so go fuck yourself.

Steve

Of course I agreed. Steve Martin was my longtime favorite. Also, Michelle would have divorced and killed me if I said no. She promptly put together her Oscars dress. I received Steve's email and she bought uncomfortable shoes within hours.

A few months later, I flew to LA for the first writers' meeting. I was scared. The other writers—Beth Armogida, Dave Boone, Andy Breckman, Jon Macks, Rita Rudner, Robert Shapiro, and Bruce Vilanch—were Hollywood comedy veterans, but I had never done anything like that.

We had a hotel convention. I later wrote about the first meeting:

Steve Martin, on my left, took notes on his laptop as the other writers brainstormed. I've always written alone, so this group process was scary. I attempted to think, but my brain was frozen into lifeless tissue. I'm sitting next to Steve Martin! was its sole coherent thought for an hour.

I realized these people were surprisingly generous, and my head began to thaw. I expected them to compete, promoting their jokes and possibly condemning others.

Nothing like that happened. The contrary was true: If someone said something excellent, the table laughed instantly and honestly; if someone said something bad, everyone sought to improve it. Many jokes evolved over time, with many people adding different aspects, until it was impossible to know whose joke it was.

Hollywood works together on most things. All these people have spent hours dreaming in writer-filled rooms like this.

By the second meeting, we loved each other and Martin's work style. His reactions to concepts were predictable. When someone made a joke, Martin would usually nod and say, "Ya, ya, ya." It meant "No." He rarely answered no because he's courteous and wanted to show the joke-teller he appreciated the effort. However, "ya" meant "no."

Martin wrote an idea into his computer when he liked it enough to consider applying it. His keyboard taptaptap was like clapping. If he loved the joke, he'd perform it, attempting several wordings and deliveries, occasionally standing up to give it the full stand-up comedy treatment. I thought Steve Martin was doing my joke if it was your idea.

I loved the Oscars, especially meeting Steve. He's brilliant and witty, but he's also serious, precise, and analytical about his work. He rehearsed the opening speech for hours, adding, cutting, and tweaking jokes until the show.

We writers, dressed in formal clothes, watched the Oscars from a small room offstage with monitors and a direct phone line to the teleprompter operator. Steve would join us after each part to discuss progress and possible revisions to upcoming content. He remained cool and attentive, constantly searching for ways to improve the show. Best Documentary Feature Oscar winner Michael Moore slammed President George W. Bush and the second Gulf War in an impassioned address. The first blatantly political scene of the show transformed the auditorium ambiance. There was booing.

Steve returned to the stage following Moore's address and a commercial break. We figured he should address it in the writers' room. I was there, but I can't describe how we made a joke in three minutes. Steve returned and remarked, "It's so sweet backstage, you should have seen it. Teamsters help Michael Moore into his limo trunk." The audience laughed, and the show continued.

It was an exciting Oscars experience. Michelle in the audience had fun too. Michelle had a great seat in front of Bono and in the same row as

Julie Andrews, one of Michelle's favorite persons, ranking slightly behind our kid but considerably above me.

After the play, we sat at Steve's table at the Governors Ball and met a procession of Hollywood stars, including Julia Roberts, who are tiny humans who never eat more than a Tic Tac. It was a great night, but Michelle's feet were in bad shape and I carried her shoes.

I wrote for Steve again in 2010, when he and Alec Baldwin cohosted the Oscars. Since then, I haven't done the Oscars, but I've had screenplays in development.

If you're new to film, let me define "a screenplay in development." We mean "a screenplay that will never become an actual movie." At least in my case.

Movie writing is completely different from my career writing. This is how you write for print—newspapers, magazines, books:

1. You write something.
2. You submit it to an editor.
3. The editor edits it.
4. It gets published.

Some of these steps may take some time. For example, the editor might want to make some changes, which you and the editor might discuss. But these four steps are essentially the process for print.

Now here, based on my experience, is the process for writing for the movie industry:

1. You write a screenplay.
2. You submit it to your agent.
3. Six months pass.
4. Your agent calls with exciting news: A company you've never heard of that is somehow connected with the movie industry has optioned your script! They want to schedule a conference call ASAP!
5. Six more months pass, during which the conference call is rescheduled four times because everybody in the movie industry is very, very busy.

6. The call finally happens. There are three to eight people on the other end. There is no way to tell. But they're excited about your screenplay. They love it! In fact they're thinking of it as a project for Tom Cruise! Who are they somehow vaguely related! Also there's a director whose name you don't recognize but they say he's very hot and he might become attached! Whatever that means! So while they're thrilled with the screenplay, they'd like you to make a few tweaks. Specifically they want you to reimagine the setting, characters, plot and overall concept. But they love it! They're eager to move forward!

7. You completely rewrite the screenplay and send it to the movie people.

8. Absolutely nothing happens for eleven months.

9. Your agent calls with good news: The movie people love the rewrite and want to have another conference call ASAP.

10. Eight more months pass, during which the follow-up conference call is rescheduled nine times.

11. You have the call. It sounds as though some, maybe most, of the movie people on this call are different from the ones who were on the first call. But whoever they are, they love the screenplay. It's perfect! However now they're thinking of it as more of an Adam Sandler vehicle. They're wondering if you can make it less Tom Cruise–y and more Adam Sandler–y.

12. You completely rewrite the screenplay.

13. A year passes, during which the follow-up conference call is rescheduled twenty-nine times.

14. You have the call. You're certain that this time you're talking to a completely different group of people. Nevertheless they love the rewrite. Here's the thing, though: They're now seeing it as more of an Emma Stone vehicle, or possibly Joe Pesci, or—thinking outside the box—a musical featuring the pig from Babe. They'd like you to have another go at it with this in mind. You try to ask "With what in mind?" But before you

can speak everyone has left the call. They're extremely busy out there.

15. You completely rewrite the screenplay with an Emma Stone/Joe Pesci–type protagonist and a subplot involving a pig that sporadically bursts into song.

16. Two to five years later you have another call. This time there's only one person on the other end. His name is Liam, and he is at most twenty years old. You can hear video game noises in the background. Liam is a senior executive in a company that bought the company that originally optioned your screenplay. He loves your screenplay, or at least the title, which is the only part he has read. He's wondering how you would feel about adapting it as an episode of a series they're developing for Hulu about competing gangs of transgender Amish flamingo breeders.

17. You completely rewrite the script.

And so on. And so. And so.

You think I exaggerate? No offense, but you've never produced a script. What I explained is the procedure. Your screenplay will be rewritten until it contains no original molecules. You do this why? You get paid. The movie industry pays generously to revise screenplays for movies they will never make.

They do this how? The business model? Without a movie, where does the money come from? I suspect many movie industry workers work in a successful business, like bathroom restoration. They're paying you to rewrite your script with money from time-consuming bathroom renovations, so it's hard to call them.

I talk authoritatively. My screenplay has been in development long enough to date Leonardo DiCaprio. Alan Zweibel, a comedy veteran and buddy, is my project partner. Original Saturday Night Live writer and cocreator of It's Garry Shandling's Show. He has worked with everyone in the company and is loved, which is impressive. His enormous skull might fit in Easter Island, but he's sensitive about it, so I'll edit this sentence later.

Alan and I wrote Lunatics, about two suburban dads who argue over an offsides call at a children's soccer game and accidentally overthrow Cuba and China, bring peace to the Middle East, and run for president of the United States.

Thus, it lacks raw realism. Wacky Romp. We sold the movie rights with a screenplay. That was 2012. We are reworking the screenplay as I type. We've done this many times, changing the plot each time. Transgender Amish flamingo breeders are the focus.

Not really. May get there before we finish.

No matter how long the process seems, I've liked working with Alan, a nice person who's simple to deal with once you get acclimated to his head size. 60 After Lunatics, Alan and I collaborated on two more books with Adam Mansbach, the author of Go the Fuck to Sleep, a lovely book of peaceful, calming poems for parents to read to their young children before bedtime.

Alan, Adam, and I wrote For This We Left Egypt? and A Field Guide to the Jews. Judaism funny books. Alan and Adam are Jewish, and I am circumcised, therefore we can write them. Three of us told Jewish jokes and two made fun of Alan's head on our fun book publicity travels.

Which takes me back to book tours, which have been a significant part of my life since my extremely unlikely Tonight Show guest appearance. That started my wild and fantastic writing career.

My literary reputation won't be as high as Marcel Proust's. Did Carson ever host Marcel Proust? Did he steal Oprah's hotel sign? Is his screenplay in progress? Do you think he wrote jokes for Steve Martin to tell at the Oscars, where Marcel Proust's widow was sitting next to Julie Andrews? Can Marcel Proust claim that his writings were adapted into a network comedy, a Broadway play, and a Zooey Deschanel-Sofia Vergara film? Has Marcel Proust ever performed "Gloria" with Bruce Springsteen backing? Was Marcel Proust circumcised?

According to my knowledge, no. I know he never joined the Remainders.

Since I started writing columns for the West Chester, Pennsylvania, Daily Local News between obituaries and regional sewage authority meetings, I've had a good run. It was a terrific run. My career has been beyond my wildest dreams.

Nothing lasts forever. Eventually, you must accept that it's over, no matter how much pleasure it was. I regret to say that time has come for me. It's over.

Regarding this chapter.

CHAPTER 8
THE END

On January 2, 2005, my Miami Herald Sunday column began:
Every writer wonders—as Shakespeare, Tolstoy, and Hemingway did—if he has any booger jokes left.

My weekly column ended, I said. I gave two arguments. My first thought was to stop before joining the group who think I was once funnier.

I still felt I was humorous. No one pressured me to stop writing my column, which was syndicated in 500 newspapers. I had the best American newspaper job.

The thing about working in comedy: Always wondering if you have it. For good reason: People are always willing to tell you you don't have it. Maybe you never had it.

My favorite humor writing quote—framed on my office wall—is from Dorothy Parker's New York Times Book assessment assessment of S. J. Perelman's The Road to Miltown:

The author's life is hard, but some purposely make it harder. In their pride and innocence, some write hilarious pieces for a living. Poor dears, the universe is rigged against them from the start since everyone can look at their work and remark, "I don't think that's funny."

Dorothy Parker was right again. As a serious opinion columnist, most readers agree or disagree. Or they don't care. No matter how they feel about your piece, they implicitly accept that you expressed an opinion as a writer.

If you're a humor writer, readers expect you to entertain them, just like comic clubgoers expect comedians to delight them. It's okay if your readers are insulted or bored to say you're bad at your job.

I'll sound whiny later, but readers have been extremely positive, loving, and sometimes even worshipful over the years. I'm grateful for my lovely, loyal readers.

Dorothy Parker highlighted that this job's occupational hazard is that anyone can judge you a failure. I've been informed in letters, emails, reviews, comments, and in person that I'm not funny or used to be funnier. People say I was funny when I wrote the Daily Local News. If I believed all those folks, my writing would be less funny than the federal tax law.

Do not believe that. I think some people dislike my writing. But I'm still funny. Those individuals are jerks.

Ha ha! Not really!

Indeed, in some situations.

My comedy is subjective, therefore it doesn't work for everyone. Fortunately, enough people liked it that I had a successful columnist career as of January 2005.

But.

But I was fifty-seven and had written a humor column for thirty years. I kept wondering, Have I told this joke before? Did I write this piece before?

I tried hard to make each column new. I knew I'd get weary of it, so I didn't want to resort to calling it in. As I said in my goodbye column, I quit before I was perceived to be funny.

That was one of my two reasons. My other goal is to work on other projects.

That includes this book and screenplays for movies that will never be made—things without a deadline. I wanted to stop thinking, "Maybe I can use this for a column," anytime I did anything, including playing dolls with my 4-year-old daughter.

Deadlines curse columnists. Columnists always consider their next column. Most of my adulthood was spent thinking about mine. I wanted to stop thinking about it. Because time is limited.

When Jeff MacNelly, the talented cartoonist who won three Pulitzer Prizes for editorial cartooning and developed the Shoe comic strip, died at fifty-two from lymphoma, I was reminded of that fact. Jeff illustrated my column for thirteen years as a friend and collaborator.

Jeff called me when I was late with a column to find out what it was about so he could illustrate it, so we talked a lot. I'd say, "I imagine it'll be about Zippy pooping on our one good rug. The rug is little. It has to be deliberate." Jeff said, "Got it." He drew a funnier comic than my piece with only that.

Jeff, a large, full-of-life guy with a great laugh, died, which shocked me. I had a life-changing conversation. I detailed this talk in Lessons from Lucy and will recap it here.

A few months after Jeff's funeral, I was on a yacht with his wife, Sue, and others who had set off a cannon to shoot his ashes into the Key West waters. After the service, I spoke with Jeff's best friend, cartoonist Mike Peters, who was at the hospital when Jeff died. Mike was surprised that the hospital staff didn't know Jeff. They thought he was Mr. MacNelly, the patient in room whatever, not a famous cartoonist with many awards.

As documented in Lessons from Lucy, Mike recognized that professional achievements are ultimately unimportant. Finally, all you have are your loved ones. Not your work, profession, honors, money, or goods. Your team.

While wealth and celebrity are good, they pale compared to family and friends.

I still think about that talk practically daily. It weighed heavily on my decision to discontinue my column. I wanted to spend less time worrying about deadlines and more time with loved ones. For twenty years, I've largely been able to do, despite the occasional deadline.

People often ask if I miss writing a weekly column. I don't, I occasionally write columns and write a lengthy Year in Review for the Herald and other periodicals.

Some readers anticipate it, while others use it to tell me I was funnier. It keeps me tied to the newspaper business, which I adore.

But the business has changed. The Internet destroyed newspapers' profitable revenue model, leading many to cut back, lay off workers, or close. Unfortunately, our caustic political rhetoric has made the news business less enjoyable.

Finally, Art Buchwald.

When my column was starting to gain national popularity in the mid-1980s, Art wrote me. That mattered to me. Art Buchwald was a Barry family staple when I was growing up. Both my parents liked him, but my mom loved him and read Herald Tribune columns aloud.

Art wrote to invite me to join the American Academy of Humor Columnists. Art wrote on academy stationery that Russell Baker, Erma Bombeck, and San Francisco Chronicle columnist Art Hoppe were all members.

I was thrilled to accept the invitation. The fact that Art just imagined and used the American Academy of Humor Columnists on his official stationery did not dampen my joy.

I was honored that he reached out to me, a newcomer to his genre. We became buddies through letters and calls. We had lunch or supper whenever he visited Miami. He was hilarious, engaging, and generous with advise.

Art's health declined in 2005. His kidneys failed and he lost a lower leg. He chose death over dialysis when his physicians informed him he needed it. In February 2006, he died in a hospice.

Instead, he lived. He should; his physicians said so. But he didn't. His million friends arrived to say goodbye and laughed with Art at the ridiculousness of the situation.

I expected a sorrowful farewell when I contacted him at hospice. Instead, he was happy and loving hospice.

He said, "I love it!" "I eat well, and everyone treats me like a million dollars."

Asking him what physicians said.

"A week or two," he said. "I could spend my life on dialysis or enjoy the sunset," he said. "I'll go to heaven," he added.

People missed his column, I told him.

"We need you," I said. "Vice president shoots people."

After laughing, we parted. I assumed that was all.

But Art kept living. After four months, he left hospice and resumed writing in June. While on Martha's Vineyard for a book event, Ridley

Pearson and I visited him at his residence in July. Joel, Art's son, led us into the room where Art had been receiving many guests.

Art, seated, greeted us and pointed to a prosthetic limb on an ottoman a few feet away.

He answered, "That's my leg." He disliked it.

We stayed for an hour as Art related his medical story, which sounds dreadful but was amusing. We embraced goodbye, and I never saw Art again.

He survived till January 2007, validating the doctors' predictions. He was honored at the Kennedy Center in March. Over 500 individuals attended, including Bob Woodward, Andy Rooney, Russell Baker, Sam Donaldson, Nancy Pelosi, and John Glenn. I spoke alongside Ben Bradlee, Tom Brokaw, Ethel Kennedy, Mike Wallace, and Art's family.

In my eulogy, I briefly mentioned my first phone call with Art, where we discussed column-writing and I felt fortunate to receive advise from a legendary figure. I wish I could comprehend him. As you know, Art spoke like he had a hamster family in his mouth."

This was true.

Art gave a video speech at his celebration. A black-tie audience watched him give a Kennedy Center monologue in 1981. Ronald Reagan laughed hysterically in the front row at Art's comments about him.

We celebrated a guy Ronald Reagan and Nancy Pelosi laughed at. Art was a Democrat who mocked government and was loved by all parties. Art, like Johnny Carson, embodied a period when political jokes were OK regardless of party.

The era is over. Many individuals today believe politics is not a joke—the stakes are too high!—and consider comedy as a tactical weapon to be used only against the other side. Some people excel at tactical political comedy. Some is hilarious. It wasn't enjoyable.

Wow, I sound old.

Art went to the Sky Big Syndicate. So have Russell Baker, Erma Bombeck, and Art Hoppe. I am the last American Academy of Humor

Columnists member. Art had all the stationery, so I never did anything official.

I'm still here. Apparently this is disputed. When you search "Is Dave Barry," Google autocomplete suggests "still alive."

I'm alive and healthy for a seventy-seven-year-old. "I'm in reasonably good health for a man of seventy-seven," means "every single organ in my body is disintegrating." At least that's my layperson interpretation of my doctors' words.

I have nearly enough physicians for a softball team, like most seniors. My heart doctor, a second heart doctor that the first heart doctor regularly sends me to for additional consultation, a kidney doctor who was referred to by the second heart doctor to determine if my kidneys could handle a certain test, which they were, but now I have to keep seeing the kidney doctor forever because apparently that is a rule; and another kidney doctor who is the brother of the first kidney doctor and sees me when his broth

I like all my physicians as people. They purposefully look for medical problems, which I think they learned in medical school, which makes me dislike them as doctors.

I try to deter them. I give my doctors nothing at doctor visits, like a Mafia boss at a congressional hearing. I answer "no" to all Patient Health History Questionnaire questions, including "What is your address?" I never admit symptoms. If I found live tadpoles in my underwear, I wouldn't tell my doctors.

They still find alarming things. This frightening conversation happens every time I see a doctor:

DOCTOR (frowning at computer screen): Your HDP level is up.

ME My what?

DOCTOR: Your hyperbolic dissimulation parameter. Last time you were at 53.7, but now you're at 61.2.

ME: Is that bad?

DOCTOR: It depends. It could mean your frenulum is having trouble extrapolating plenary acids.

ME: Is that bad?

DOCTOR: It depends. It can lead to CDFV.

ME: To what?

DOCTOR: Catastrophic devolution of the fiduciary viaduct.

ME: Is that bad?

DOCTOR: In 30 percent of the cases it's fatal.

ME: What about the other 70 percent?

DOCTOR: They're also fatal.

ME: So I'm going to die?

DOCTOR: It depends.

I always require more tests after these chats, which gives the doctor something to worry about and maybe a new doctor for me to hire. Doctors seldom say, "Everything looks great, Dave!" See you in 5-10 years!"

Of course my circumstance isn't unique: Most in my age group is sick. Baby Boomers—the generation that endured the Great Depression, won World War II, and landed a man on the moon—are dying.

That wasn't us. Our generation partied naked for three days on LSD and dirt at Woodstock. We read bottled water components now, but we were young and reckless then. Providing we can find our reading glasses.

Boomers are old. The race is almost over. We must pass on our expertise and experience to the next generation.

Unfortunately, younger generations don't want our advice. Gen X, Millennials, and Gen Z agree that Boomers should shut up.

This makes sense. Much of the advice Boomers pass on to subsequent generations sounds like this:

"Your music sucks."

"Why are you always looking at your phone?"

"No melody! Just people shouting!"

"We didn't have cell phones when I was your age!"

"You'll regret those tattoos someday."

"We had no Instagram or TikTok!"

"You'd be so much prettier without that stupid ring in your nose."

We had no influencers!

"If you didn't waste money on Starbucks, you could buy a house."
We lacked blah!"
Blah blah!"
And so on. Boomer wisdom is mostly grumbling, the senescent venting of a generation that has aged like the others.

This is my fault. If my daughter tells me she was at a concert with a celebrity DJ, I will reflexively rant about how stupid the term "celebrity DJ" is, because we're talking about a person who plays records, which requires no more musical talent than using a toaster oven. Why do people act like this person is a Jimi Hendrix-level virtuoso when he's just a headphone?

I realize how hopelessly old I sound telling these things. Since my kid has heard this rant many times, her eyes show pity. I repeat anyway. My Boomer truth must be spoken!

As the lawfully chosen spokesperson for my generation, do I have any true knowledge to share? Have I learned anything worth passing on? Maybe.

I listed twenty-five things I'd learnt by fifty years old. Some of them were jokes. As an example:

- If you had to identify, in one word, the reason why the human race has not achieved, and never will achieve, its full potential, that word would be: "meetings."
- You should never say anything to a woman that even remotely suggests you think she's pregnant unless you can see an actual baby emerging from her at that moment.
- The one thing that unites all human beings, regardless of age, gender, religion, economic status or ethnic background, is that, deep down inside, we all believe that we are above-average drivers.
- There is a very fine line between "hobby" and "mental illness."

But some of my twenty-five things were sincere attempts to express life lessons. Five of those things still strike me as fundamentally true, and worth passing along:

You should not confuse your career with your life.

A person who is nice to you, but rude to the waiter, is not a nice person.
No matter what happens, somebody will find a way to take it too seriously.
Your friends love you anyway.
Nobody cares if you can't dance well. Just get up and dance.
But some of my twenty-five things were sincere attempts to express life lessons. Five of those things still strike me as fundamentally true, and worth passing along:

1. You should not confuse your career with your life.
2. A person who is nice to you, but rude to the waiter, is not a nice person.
3. No matter what happens, somebody will find a way to take it too seriously.
4. Your friends love you anyway.
5. Nobody cares if you can't dance well. Just get up and dance.

I pass those five nuggets on to future generations who will listen to a DJ-dissing old fart.
One more wisdom tidbit, becoming increasingly true with age: It'll be OK.
That means:
Some Very Bad Thing has been predicted my whole life. I was informed nuclear war was coming. I've heard that global cooling and warming will make the world uninhabitable. We were informed we would run out of food, oil, and water. A pandemic will destroy society, I've heard. Multiple people have warned me of a global economic disaster. I was told communists and fascists will take control the US government. People say breakdancing will be an Olympic sport eventually.
That last one happened. However, some did not. For 80 years, I've heard catastrophic prophecies, typically from authority. If I'd believed all these forecasts, I'd have lived in constant fear.

Thank goodness I didn't. Most didn't. Most of us lived as if life would continue. Our kids have kids because they expect life to continue, just like we did.

Does that mean nothing catastrophic ever happens? No. Should you avoid learning about climate change? Again, no. Spending all your days worrying about some dreadful tragedy that never happens wastes your only days.

Because fostering fear is beneficial, they will always tell you to be terrified. Most big faiths capitalize on scaring you with entire enterprises. Both major political parties generate millions by saying we're doomed if the other party wins. Journalists enjoy explaining why to be afraid.

Life carries on. It did for my generation and will for yours. So when the next Very Bad Thing hits and panic sets in, remember: It'll be OK. As you may recall, this book is about my life's wisdom. My life continues as I type, but the book is almost ended. Despite my softball team of doctors' reservations, I hope it lasts.

Everyone dies, possibly except Keith Richards. When you reach my age, you naturally consider your own demise. When will it happen? It will happen how? Will you die with dignity in clean jammies or Elvis-style on the toilet in midpoop? Will your final words to loved ones be sensible and memorable or "Glurg"? What will your obituary say? Will it list your life achievements other than International Talk Like a Pirate Day, which you didn't start?

I don't know these answers. I have a sense of what death would be like. Yes, I've been a corpse.

In 1994, I wrote a column arguing that opera could kill humans:

I base this statement on an Associated Press article, sent in by many alert readers, concerning an alarming incident in Denmark involving an okapi, which is a rare African mammal related to the giraffe. The article states that this okapi—I am not making this quotation up—"died from stress apparently triggered by opera singers."

The okapi was not actually attending an opera when this happened. It was in a zoo 300 yards from a park where opera singers were rehearsing. A zoo spokesperson was quoted as saying that okapis "can be severely affected by unusual sounds."

So here are the essential facts:

1. *An okapi, minding its own business, was killed by opera music being sung three football fields away.*
2. *Okapis are members of the mammal family.*
3. *Most humans`, not counting Congress, are also members of the mammal family.*

When I consider these facts together, a very disturbing question comes to my mind, as I'm sure it does yours: What were three football fields doing in Denmark?

Another question is: Could opera, in sufficient dosages, also be fatal to human beings?

I decided that the federal government may have to ban opera for public health reasons. Although I was joking, some opera fans took offense. I received some of the harshest hate mail from that column. In response to my incorrect opera remarks, one writer stated that "Così Fan Tutte is Italian, not Spanish, you cocksucker." Fuck you."

I received a great letter about that column. It came from Eugene Opera general manager Janice Mackey. She offered to cast me as a corpse in Gianni Schicchi.

Of course I agreed. A follow-up column stated, "I am always looking for new ways to get paid for being motionless."

I went to Eugene, which is difficult from Miami:

To get there, you have to take a series of "commuter" airplanes, each one smaller than the last, until finally there isn't room for both you and the pilot, and you have to fly yourself. "Eugene is that way!" the airline personnel tell you, gesturing vaguely. "Just look for the rain cloud!"

The Eugene Opera staff was amazing. Not much fun being a corpse. They made me wear irritating tights, an old-man nightshirt, a wig, and extensive makeup. Then I had to lie in a bed onstage under bright lights and hold still—dead men don't scratch—while a squadron of professional opera singers with vocal cords like tram cables bellowed in a foreign language for 45 minutes at close range without inhaling.

According to my corpse experience, death is noisy. Also itchy. It was unpleasant. I won't die again unless necessary.

That's my memoir. Thanks for reading. You know where I obtained my ideas (Costco) and all about my life at 77. If anything important occurs to me, I may be legally compelled to write another memoir, which I want to avoid. From now on, I aim to live a calm, event-free existence as I slowly approach eighty and beyond.

I think it'll be fine.

Printed in Dunstable, United Kingdom